It's another Quality Book from CGP

This book is for anyone doing GCSE Mathematics at Foundation Level.

It contains lots of tricky questions designed
to make you sweat — because that's the only
way you'll get any better.

It's also got some daft bits in to try and make
the whole experience at least vaguely
entertaining for you.

What CGP is all about

Our sole aim here at CGP is to produce the highest quality
books — carefully written, immaculately presented and
dangerously close to being funny.

Then we work our socks off to get them out to you
— at the cheapest possible prices.

Contents

Section Five

Handling Data

Section Six

Graphs

Section Seven

Algebra

Throughout the book, the more challenging questions are marked like this: **Q1** .

Published by Coordination Group Publications Ltd.
Illustrated by Ruso Bradley, Lex Ward and Ashley Tyson

From original material by Richard Parsons.

Contributors:

Gill Allen	C McLoughlin
Margaret Carr	Gordon Rutter
Barbara Coleman	John Waller
JE Dodds	Dave Williams
Mark Haslam	Philip Wood
John Lyons	

Updated by:
Simon Little, Ali Palin and Emma Stevens

With thanks to Dominic Hall *and*
Peter Caunter *for the proofreading.*

ISBN: 978 1 84146 553 1

Groovy website: www.cgpbooks.co.uk

Printed by Elanders Ltd, Newcastle upon Tyne.
Clipart sources: CorelDRAW® and VECTOR.

Ordering Numbers and Place Value

Q1   Put these numbers in ascending (smallest to biggest) order.

a) 23   117   5   374   13   89   67   54   716   18

....

b) 1272   231   817   376   233   46   2319   494   73   1101

....

Q2   Write down the value of the number 4 in each of these.

For example   408 ....*hundreds*........

a) 347 ....

b) 41 ....

c) 5478 ....

d) 6754 ....

e) 4897 ....

f) 6045 ....

g) 64098 ....

h) 745320 ....

i) 405759 ....

j) 2402876 ....

k) 4987321 ....

l) 6503428 ....

Q3   Put these numbers in order of size — from the smallest to the largest.

a) 3.42   4.23   2.43   3.24   2.34   4.32

....

b) 6.7   6.704   6.64   6.642   6.741

....

> Always look at the whole number part first, then the first digit after the decimal point, then the next etc.

c) 1002.8   102.8   1008.2   1020.8   108.2

....

Multiplying by 10, 100, etc.

Multiplying by 10, 100 or 1000 moves each digit 1, 2 or 3 places to the left —
you just fill the rest of the space with zeros.

Fill in the missing numbers. Do not use a calculator for this page.

no calculators!!

Q1 **a)** $6 \times \boxed{} = 60$ **b)** $0.07 \times \boxed{} = 0.7$

c) $6 \times \boxed{} = 600$ **d)** $0.07 \times \boxed{} = 7$

e) $6 \times \boxed{} = 6000$ **f)** $0.07 \times \boxed{} = 70$

Q2   Which number is ten times as large as 25?   ....

Q3   Which number is one hundred times as large as 93?   ....

Q4 **a)** $8 \times 10 =$ ....   **b)** $34 \times 100 =$ ....   **c)** $52 \times 100 =$ ....

d) $9 \times 1000 =$ ....   **e)** $436 \times 1000 =$ ....   **f)** $0.2 \times 10 =$ ....

g) $6.9 \times 10 =$ ....   **h)** $4.73 \times 100 =$ ....

Q5   For a school concert chairs are put out in rows of 10.
How many will be needed for 16 rows?   ....

Q6      How much do 10 chickens cost?   ....

£2.99
EACH

Q7   A school buys calculators for £2.45 each.
How much will 100 cost?   ....

Q8   A shop bought 1000 bars of chocolate for £0.43 each.
How much did they cost altogether?   ....

Q9 **a)** $20 \times 30 =$ ....   **b)** $40 \times 700 =$ ....   **c)** $250 \times 20 =$ ....

d) $6000 \times 210 =$ ....   **e)** $18000 \times 500 =$ ....

Dividing by 10, 100, etc.

Dividing by 10, 100 or 1000 moves each digit 1, 2 or 3 places to the right.

Answer these questions <u>without</u> using a calculator:

Q1 **a)** 30 ÷ 10 = ...

b) 43 ÷ 10 = ...

c) 5.8 ÷ 10 = ...

d) 63.2 ÷ 10 = ...

e) 0.5 ÷ 10 = ...

f) 400 ÷ 100 = ...

g) 423 ÷ 100 = ...

h) 228.6 ÷ 100 = ...

i) 61.5 ÷ 100 = ...

j) 2.96 ÷ 100 = ...

k) 6000 ÷ 1000 = ...

l) 6334 ÷ 1000 = ...

m) 753.6 ÷ 1000 = ...

n) 8.15 ÷ 1000 = ...

o) 80 ÷ 20 = ...

p) 860 ÷ 20 = ...

q) 2400 ÷ 300 = ...

r) 480 ÷ 40 = ...

s) 860 ÷ 200 = ...

t) 63.9 ÷ 30 = ...

Q2 Ten people share a Lottery win of £62.
How much should each person receive?

....

Q3 Blackpool Tower is 158 m tall. If a model
of it is built to a scale of 1 : 100, how tall
would the model be?

....

Q4 If 1000 identical ball-bearings weigh 2100 g,
what is the weight of one of the ball-bearings?

....

Q5 Mark went on holiday to France. He exchanged £200 for 320 euros to spend while he
was there. How many euros did he get for each £1?

....

4

Adding

Q1 Do these questions as quickly as you can:

a) 63
       +32

b) 75
        +48

c) 528
        +196

Q2 Now try these, writing the answers in the spaces provided:

a) 5 + 9

b) 26 + 15

c) 34 + 72

= ....

= ....

= ....

d) 238 + 56

e) 528 + 173

f) 215 + 2514

= ....

= ....

= ....

Q3 Add the rows and add the columns:

a)

2	6	7	
8	6	4	
4	2	9	

b)

8	3	7	
2	6	9	
7	3	4	

c)

2	7	1	
6	5	8	
3	6	2	

Q4 Boxes in a music warehouse contain the following numbers of CDs:

62	218	894	42
361	1283	59	732
54	745	29	319

Select the three boxes that contain the most CDs.
How many CDs will you have?
Put your answer in the shaded box.

			Total

Select the three boxes that contain the least number of CDs.
How many do you have now?
Put your answer in the shaded box.

			Total

Subtracting

Answer the following questions <u>without</u> using a calculator.

Q1 Subtract the following:

    a)   36
          −13

    b)   45
          −23

    c)   89
          −24

    d)   25
         − 8

    e)   80
          −42

    f)   72
         −19

Q2 Now subtract these:

    a) 687 − 235

    b) 754 − 538

    c) 843 − 516

    d) 634 − 98

    = ...

    = ...

    = ...

    = ...

    e) 908 − 325

    f) 650 − 317

    g) 830 − 293

    h) 700 − 248

    = ...

    = ...

    = ...

    = ...

Q3 Scafell Pike is 979 m high. Ben Nevis is 1344 m high.
What is the difference in height between the two mountains?

    The word 'difference' tells you it's a subtraction question.

               ....

Q4 Fill in the missing digits:

    a)   6 5
         −3 •
          • 4

    b)   7 3 •
        −2 • 4
         • 2 5

    c)   8 7 •
       − • 3 2
        2 • 9

    d)   • 5 6
       −2 7 8
       1 • •

Adding Decimals

Q1 Work out the answers without using a calculator.

a)   2.4
     +3.2

b)   3.5
     +4.6

c)   6.2
     + 5.9

d)   7.34
     + 6.07

e)   9.08
     +4.93

f)   1 5.73
     +25.08

g)   26.05
     + 72.95

Q2 Write these out in columns and work out the answers without using a calculator.

a) 3.6 + 7.3   **b)** 21.4 + 13.8   **c)** 0.9 + 5.6   **d)** 9.98 + 6.03   **e)** 2.9 + 7

f) 4.36 + 7.1   **g)** 9.8 + 1.05   **h)** 6 + 6.75   **i)** 0.28 + 18.5   **j)** 47.23 + 6.7

Q3 Work out the missing lengths without using a calculator.

a)

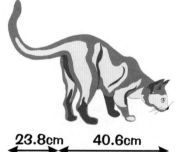

23.8cm   40.6cm

?cm

b)

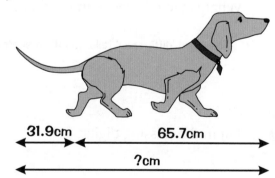

31.9cm   65.7cm

?cm

Subtracting Decimals

Q1 Work these out <u>without</u> a calculator:

a) 9.8
−3.1

b) 7.3
−2.3

c) 6.2
−1.5

d) 8.6
−3.9

e) 7.0
−1.6

f) 13.6
−12.7

g) 14.65
−4.7

h) 8.34
−4.65

Q2 Put the following in columns first, then work them out without using a calculator:

a) 8.5 – 1.6

b) 18.3 – 5.9

c) 24.1 – 16.3

> You have to give the whole numbers a decimal point yourself... and some zeros too. E.g. 9 – 3.6 becomes 9.0 – 3.6.

d) 9 – 3.6

e) 40 – 2.3

f) 51 – 18.32

Answer questions 3 and 4 without using a calculator.

Q3 Kate bought a jar of coffee for £3.24 and paid for it with a £5 note.
How much change should she get?

> When you're dealing with money, you've got two decimal places.

....

Q4 Work out the height of the table which the television is standing on.

0.48m

1.18m

?

....

Multiplying

Q1   Multiply the following <u>without</u> a calculator:

a) 23×2 **b)** 40×3 **c)** 53×4

= ....   = ...   = ...

d) 13×5 **e)** 25×4 **f)** 42×3

= ....   = ...   = ...

g) 18×2 **h)** 54×3 **i)** 75×5 **j)** 93×4

= ....   = ...   = ...   = ...

k) 308×4 **l)** 825×3 **m)** 346×5 **n)** 286×6

= ....   = ...   = ...   = ...

o) 126×14 **p)** 413×26 **q)** 309×61 **r)** 847×53

= ....   = ...   = ...   = ...

Q2   Without using a calculator, work out the total cost of 6 pens at 54p each.

....

Q3   Without using a calculator, calculate how many hours
there are in a year (365 days).

....

Dividing

no calculators!!

Do these division questions <u>without</u> a calculator:

Q1 **a)** 46 ÷ 2   You may wish to set the sum out like this

$$2\overline{)46}^{\,23}$$

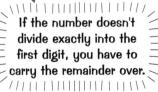

b) 86 ÷ 2   **c)** 96 ÷ 3   **d)** 76 ÷ 4

If the number doesn't divide exactly into the first digit, you have to carry the remainder over.

e) 85 ÷ 5   **f)** 96 ÷ 6   **g)** 91 ÷ 7

Q2   Try these:

a) 834 ÷ 3   **b)** 645 ÷ 5   **c)** 702 ÷ 6

d) 900 ÷ 4   **e)** 1000 ÷ 8   **f)** 747 ÷ 9

Q3   Seven people share a lottery win of £868.00. How much does each person get?

....

Q4   A chocolate cake containing 944 calories is split into 8 slices.
How many calories are in each slice?

....

Multiplying Decimals

A good way to multiply decimals is to ignore the decimal point to start with — just multiply
the numbers. Then put the point back in and CHECK your answer looks sensible.

Do these calculations <u>without</u> using a calculator:

Q1 **a)** 3.2 × 4   **b)** 8.3 × 5   **c)** 6.4 × 3

= ....   = ...   = ...

d) 21 × 0.3   **e)** 263 × 0.2   **f)** 2.4 × 3.1

= ....   = ...   = ...

Q2 At a petrol station each pump shows a ready reckoner table. Complete the table when
the cost of unleaded petrol is 94.9p per litre.

Litres	Cost in pence
1	94.9
5	
10	
20	
50	

Q3 Jason can run 5.3 metres in 2 seconds. How far will he run if he
keeps up this pace for:

a) 20 seconds   **b)** 60 seconds   **c)** 5 minutes

....

Carl can run 7.4 metres in 2 seconds. How far will he run if
he keeps up this pace for:

d) 20 seconds   **e)** 60 seconds   **f)** 5 minutes

....

g) If they both keep up their pace for half an hour how far will each of them run?

Jason will run .... metres.

Carl will run .... metres.

Dividing Decimals

 This is the same thing, really — you divide the numbers first, then you put in the point where it should be.

Q1 Divide these without a calculator.

a) 8.4 ÷ 2   You may wish to set the sum out like this

$$2\overline{\smash{)}8.4}\ ^{4.2}$$

b) 7.5 ÷ 3   **c)** 8.5 ÷ 5   **d)** 26.6 ÷ 7

e) 6.2 ÷ 5   **f)** 2.3 ÷ 4   **g)** 0.9 ÷ 5

Q2 Try these without a calculator:

a) 2.06 ÷ 8   **b)** 0.405 ÷ 6   **c)** 0.3 ÷ 8

d) 4.75 ÷ 5   **e)** 8.28 ÷ 9   **f)** 0.944 ÷ 8

No calculators allowed for these two either:

Q3 Eight people share £9.36 equally. How much does each get?

....

Q4 A plank of wood 8.34 m long is cut into 6 equal pieces.
How long is each piece?

....

Special Number Sequences

There are five special sequences: EVEN, ODD, SQUARE, CUBE and TRIANGLE NUMBERS. You really need to know them and their n^{th} terms.

EVEN   SQUARE   ODD   CUBE   TRIANGLE

Q1   What are these sequences called, and what are their next 3 terms?

a) 2, 4, 6, 8, …

....

b) 1, 3, 5, 7, …

....

c) 1, 4, 9, 16, …

....

d) 1, 8, 27, 64, …

....

e) 1, 3, 6, 10, …

....

Q2   The following sequences are described in words. Write down their first four terms.

a) The prime numbers starting from 37.

....

b) The powers of 2 starting from 32.

....

c) The squares of odd numbers starting from $7^2 = 49$.

....

d) The powers of 10 starting from 1000.

....

e) The triangular numbers starting from 15.   *The nth term is ½ n(n + 1) — you're starting from n = 5.*

....

Multiples

The multiples of a number are its times table — if you need multiples of more than one number, do them separately then pick the ones in both lists.

Q1 What are the first five multiples of:

a) 4? ....

b) 7? ....

c) 12? ....

d) 18? ....

Q2 Find a number which is a multiple of:

A quick way to do these is just to multiply the numbers together.

a) 2 and 6 ....

b) 7 and 5 ....

c) 2 and 3 and 7 ....

d) 4 and 5 and 9 ....

Q3 **a)** Find a number which is a multiple of 3 and 8 ....

b) Find another number which is a multiple of 3 and 8 ....

c) Find another number which is a multiple of 3 and 8 ....

Q4 Which of these numbers 14, 20, 22, 35, 50, 55, 70, 77, 99 are multiples of:

a) 2? ....

b) 5? ....

c) 7? ....

d) 11? ....

Factors

Factors multiply together to make other numbers.

E.g. $1 \times 6 = 6$ and $2 \times 3 = 6$, so 6 has factors 1, 2, 3 and 6.

Q1 These are the hands of aliens. Each alien has a times sum on each finger. The answer to each finger is the same and is the number by which that species is known.

When Sculder & Mulley found the following aliens they had all their fingers but were missing their factor sums. Write in each sum and the alien species number.

Q2 The numbers on each finger are known as factors and are usually, on Earth, written as a list. List the factors of the following numbers. Each factor is written once, no repeats.

a) 18 ....

b) 22 ....

c) 35 ....

d) 7 ....

e) 16 ....

f) 49 ....

g) 48 ....

h) 31 ....

i) 50 ....

j) 62 ....

k) 81 ....

l) 100 ....

Factors

Q3 a) I am a factor of 24.
I am an odd number.
I am bigger than 1.
What number am I?

....

b) I am a factor of 30.
I am an even number.
I am less than 5.
What number am I?

....

Q4   Circle all the factors of 360 in this list of numbers.

    1   2   3   4   5   6   7   8   9   10

Q5   A perfect number is one where the factors add up to the number itself.
For example, the factors of 28 are 1, 2, 4, 7 and 14 (not including 28 itself).
These add up to 1 + 2 + 4 + 7 + 14 = 28, and so 28 is a perfect number.

Complete this table, and circle the perfect number in the left hand column.

Number	Factors (excluding the number itself)	Sum of Factors
2		
4	1, 2	3
6		
8		
10		

The sum of the factors is all the factors added together.

Q6 a) What is the biggest number that is a factor of both 42 and 18?

....

b) What is the smallest number that has both 4 and 18 as factors?

....

Q7   Complete the factor trees below to express each number as a product of prime factors.
The first one has been done for you.

60

2 × 30

2 × 15

3 × 5

60 = 2×2×3×5

88

2 × ☐

2 × ☐

☐ × ☐

88 = 2×2×.........×.........

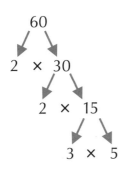

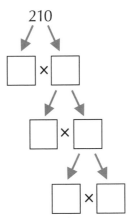

210

☐ × ☐

☐ × ☐

☐ × ☐

210 = ... × .... × .... × ....

LCM and HCF

The Lowest Common Multiple (LCM) is the **SMALLEST** number that will **DIVIDE BY ALL** the numbers in question.

The Highest Common Factor (HCF) is the **BIGGEST** number that will **DIVIDE INTO ALL** the numbers in question.

Q1 **a)** List the <u>first ten</u> multiples of 6, <u>starting at 6</u>.

....

b) List the <u>first ten</u> multiples of 5, <u>starting at 5</u>.

....

c) What is the <u>LCM</u> of 5 and 6?

....

Q2 For each set of numbers find the HCF.

a) 3, 5 **c)** 10, 15 **e)** 14, 21

....

b) 6, 8 **d)** 27, 48 **f)** 11, 33, 121

....

Q3 For each set of numbers, find the LCM.

a) 3, 5 **c)** 10, 15 **e)** 14, 21

....

b) 6, 8 **d)** 15, 18 **f)** 11, 33, 44

....

Q4 Lars, Rita and Alan regularly go swimming. Lars goes every 2 days, Rita goes every 3 days and Alan goes every 5 days. They <u>all</u> went swimming together on Friday 1st June.

This is a LCM question in disguise.

a) On what <u>date</u> will Lars and Rita next go swimming together?

....

b) On what <u>date</u> will Rita and Alan next go swimming together?

....

c) On what <u>day of the week</u> will all 3 next go swimming together?

....

d) Which of the 3 (if any) will go swimming on 15th June?

....

Prime Numbers

Basically, prime numbers don't divide by anything (except 1 and themselves).
5 is prime — it will only divide by 1 or 5. 1 is an exception to this rule — it is not prime.

Q1 Write down the first ten prime numbers. ....

Q2 Give a reason for 27 not being a prime number. ....

Q3 Using any or all of the figures **1, 2, 3, 7** write down:

   a) the smallest prime number ....

   b) a prime number greater than 20 ....

   c) a prime number between 10 and 20 ....

   d) two prime numbers whose sum is 20 .... , ...

   e) a number that is not prime. ....

Q4 Find all the prime numbers between 40 and 50. ....

Q5 In the <u>ten by ten square</u> opposite, ring all the prime numbers.

The first three have been done for you.

1	②	③	4	⑤	6	7	8	9	10
11	12	13	14	15	16	17	18	19	20
21	22	23	24	25	26	27	28	29	30
31	32	33	34	35	36	37	38	39	40
41	42	43	44	45	46	47	48	49	50
51	52	53	54	55	56	57	58	59	60
61	62	63	64	65	66	67	68	69	70
71	72	73	74	75	76	77	78	79	80
81	82	83	84	85	86	87	88	89	90
91	92	93	94	95	96	97	98	99	100

Q6 A school ran three evening classes: <u>judo, karate and kendo</u>.
The judo class had 29 pupils, the karate class had 27 and the kendo class 23.
For which classes would the teacher have difficulty dividing the pupils into equal groups?

....

Q7 Find three sets of three prime numbers which add up to the following numbers:

10 ..../ ..../ ....   **29** ..../ ..../ ....   **41** ..../ ..../ ....

Ratio

Ratios compare quantities of the same kind — so if the units aren't mentioned, they've got to be the same in each bit of the ratio.

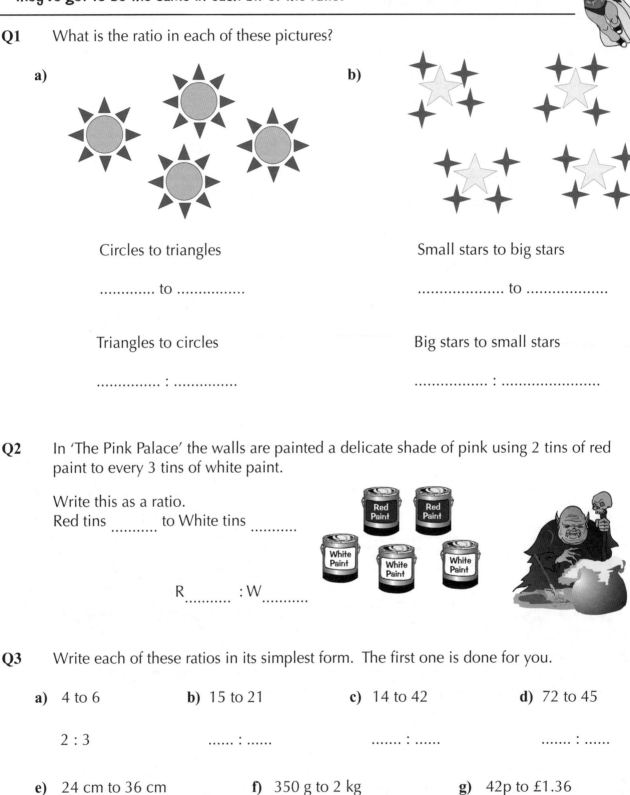

Q1 What is the ratio in each of these pictures?

a)

Circles to triangles

.... to ....

Triangles to circles

.... : ....

b)

Small stars to big stars

.... to ....

Big stars to small stars

.... : ....

Q2 In 'The Pink Palace' the walls are painted a delicate shade of pink using 2 tins of red paint to every 3 tins of white paint.

Write this as a ratio.
Red tins .... to White tins ....

R.......... : W..........

Q3 Write each of these ratios in its simplest form. The first one is done for you.

a) 4 to 6   **b)** 15 to 21   **c)** 14 to 42   **d)** 72 to 45

2 : 3   ...... : .... : .... : ......

e) 24 cm to 36 cm   **f)** 350 g to 2 kg   **g)** 42p to £1.36

...... : .... : .... : ......

Watch out for ones like f) and g) — you need to make the units the same first.

SECTION ONE — NUMBERS

Ratio

I think I can spot a Golden Rule lurking here...
DIVIDE FOR ONE, THEN TIMES FOR ALL.

Q4 To make grey paint, black and white paint are mixed in the ratio 5:3. How much black paint would be needed with:

a) 6 litres of white? ....

b) 12 litres of white? ....

c) 21 litres of white? ....

Q5 To make orange squash you mix water and concentrated orange juice in the ratio 9:2. How much water is needed with:

a) 10 ml of concentrated juice? ....

b) 30 ml of concentrated juice? ....

c) 42 ml of concentrated juice? ....

Q6 The ratio of men to women at a football match was 11:4.
How many men were there if there were:

a) 2000 women? ....

b) 8460 women? ....

How many women were there if there were:

c) 22000 men? ....

d) 6820 men? ....

Ratio

Q7 Divide the following quantities in the given ratio.

For example:

£400 in the ratio 1 : 4   1 + 4 = 5   £400 ÷ 5 = £80

<u>1 × £80 = £80 and 4 × £80 = £320</u>   <u>£80 : £320</u>

a) 100 g in the ratio 1 : 4   .... + ... = ... ÷ .... = ...

.... × .... = ... and .... × .... = ...

= .... : ....

b) 500 m in the ratio 2 : 3 = ... : ....

c) £12000 in the ratio 1 : 2 = ... : ....

d) 6.3 kg in the ratio 3 : 4 = ... : ....

e) £8.10 in the ratio 4 : 5 = ... : ....

Q8 Now try these…

a) Adam and Mags win £24 000. They split the money in the ratio 1 : 5. How much does Adam get?

....

b) Sunil and Paul compete in a pizza eating contest. Between them they consume 28 pizzas in the ratio 3 : 4. Who wins and how many did they eat?

.... eats .... pizzas

c) The total distance covered in a triathlon (swimming, cycling and running) is 15 km. It is split in the ratio 2 : 3 : 5. How far is each section?

Swimming = ..., cycling = ..., running = ...

A great way to check your answer works is to add up the individual quantities — they should add up to the original amount.

Best Buys

Start by finding the **AMOUNT PER PENNY** — the more
of the stuff you get per penny, the better value it is.

Q1

The small bar of chocolate weighs 50 g and costs 32p.
The large bar weighs 200 g and costs 80p.

a) How many grams do you get for 1p from the small bar?

....

b) How many grams do you get for 1p from the large bar?

....

c) Which bar gives you more for your money?

....

Q2 The large tin of tuna weighs 400 g and costs £1.05.
The small tin weighs 220 g and costs 57p.

a) How many grams do you get for 1p in the large tin?

....

b) How many grams do you get for 1p in the small tin?

....

c) Which tin gives better value for money?

....

Q3 Which of these boxes of eggs is better value for money?

60p ....

£1.10 ....

Fragtions

  This circle is divided into two equal parts — each bit is 1/2 of the whole.

Q1 What fraction is shaded in each of the following pictures?

a)

b)

c)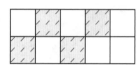

d)

....

e)

f)

g)

....

Q2 Shade the diagram to show the following fractions.

a) $\dfrac{3}{8}$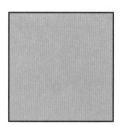

b) $\dfrac{2}{5}$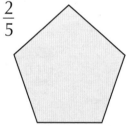

c) $\dfrac{7}{10}$

Q3 There are 32 boxes of shoes stacked on a shelf.

If five eighths are sold, show on the diagram how many are left.

Fractions

To make an **EQUIVALENT** fraction, you've got to multiply the **TOP** (numerator) and **BOTTOM** (denominator) by the **SAME THING**.

Q4 Shade in the correct number of sections to make these diagrams equivalent.

 $\frac{1}{4} =$

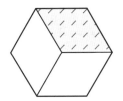 $\frac{1}{3} =$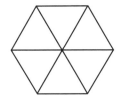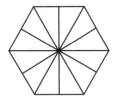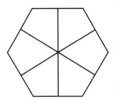

Q5 Write in the missing numbers to make these fractions equivalent.

For example 1/2 = 7/14

a) 1/4 = 4/........

b) 3/4 = 9/........

c) 1/3 = ... /6

d) 2/3 = 8/........

e) 2/7 = 6/........

f) 6/18 = 1/........

g) 8/16 = ... /2

h) 24/32 = 3/........

i) 10/60 = 5/........

Q6 Write in the missing numbers to make each list equivalent.

a) 1/2 = 2/...... = ... /6 = ... /8 = 5/10 = 25/...... = ... /70 = ... /100

b) 200/300 = 100/...... = ... /15 = 40/...... = 120/180 = ... /9 = ... /3

c) 7/10 = 14/...... = ... /30 = 210/...... = 49/...... = ... /20

d) 19/20 = ... /80 = 38/...... = 57/...... = ... /100 = ... /1000

e) 500/600 = 250/...... = 50/...... = ... /150 = 1000/......

Q7 Which is bigger?

a) 1/5 or 2/10 ....

b) 3/7 or 6/21 ....

c) 10/15 or 4/6 ....

d) 1/3 or 33/100 ....

Fractions of Quantities

Q1 Write down the following quantities:

a) Half of 12 = ...

b) Quarter of 24 = ...

c) Third of 30 = ...

d) 1/4 of 44 = ...

e) 3/4 of 60 = ...

f) 2/3 of 6 = ...

Q2 Calculate the fractions of the following:

eg. 1/3 of 18 = 18 ÷ 3 = <u>6</u>

a) 1/8 of 32 = ... ÷ 8 = ...

b) 1/10 of 50 = ... ÷ 10 = ...

c) 1/12 of 144 = ... ÷ .... = ...

d) 1/25 of 75 = ... ÷ .... = ...

e) 1/30 of 180 = ... ÷ .... = ...

f) 1/27 of 540 = ... ÷ .... = ...

Q3 Calculate the fractions of the following:

eg. 2/5 of 50   50 ÷ 5 = 10   2 × 10 = <u>20</u>

a) 2/3 of 60   60 ÷ 3 = ...   2 × .... = ...

b) 4/5 of 25   25 ÷ .... = ...   4 × .... = ...

c) 7/9 of 63   .... ÷ .... = ... × .... = ...

d) 3/10 of 100   .... ÷ .... = ... × .... = ...

e) 12/19 of 760   .... ÷ .... = ... × .... = ...

f) 6/9 of £1.80   .... ÷ .... = ... × .... = £........ or .... p

g) 10/18 of £9.00   .... ÷ .... = ... × .... = £........

h) 2/3 of one day (24 hours)   .... ÷ .... = ... × .... = ... hours

i) 5/6 of one year (12 months)   .... ÷ .... = ... × .... = ... months

j) 2/5 of one kilogram (1000 grams)   .... = ... g

Fraction Arithmetic

Fraction arithmetic becomes a nice cruise in the park, once you've learned the rules for dealing with each type of sum.

> **MULTIPLYING:** just multiply the <u>tops</u> and the <u>bottoms</u>.
> **DIVIDING:** turn the second fraction <u>upside down</u>, then <u>multiply them</u>.
>
> **ADDING OR SUBTRACTING:**
> 1) Make the bottom number <u>the same</u> (get "a common denominator")
> 2) Add or subtract the top numbers <u>only</u>.

Answer the following questions <u>without</u> using a calculator.

Q1   Change these top-heavy fractions to mixed numbers:

a) $\frac{3}{2} =$ .... **b)** $\frac{7}{4} =$ .... **c)** $\frac{8}{3} =$ ....

For some of the questions below, you'll need to change the mixed fractions into top-heavy fractions at the start.

Change these mixed numbers to top-heavy fractions:

d) $2\frac{1}{2} =$ .... **e)** $3\frac{1}{3} =$ .... **f)** $1\frac{3}{5} =$ ....

Q2   Do the following multiplications, expressing the answers as fractions in their lowest terms:

a) $\frac{4}{3} \times \frac{3}{4}$ ....

d) $2\frac{1}{2} \times \frac{3}{5}$ ....

b) $\frac{2}{5} \times \frac{3}{4}$ ....

e) $10\frac{2}{7} \times \frac{7}{9}$ ....

c) $\frac{11}{9} \times \frac{6}{5}$ ....

f) $2\frac{1}{6} \times 3\frac{1}{3}$ ....

Q3   Carry out the following divisions, and express each answer in its lowest terms:

a) $\frac{1}{4} \div \frac{3}{8}$ ....

d) $1\frac{1}{2} \div \frac{5}{12}$ ....

b) $\frac{1}{9} \div \frac{2}{3}$ ....

e) $10\frac{4}{5} \div \frac{9}{10}$ ....

c) $\frac{15}{24} \div \frac{6}{5}$ ....

f) $3\frac{7}{11} \div 1\frac{4}{11}$ ....

Q4   Add the two fractions, giving your answer as a fraction in its lowest terms:

a) $\frac{7}{8} + \frac{3}{8}$ ....

b) $\frac{1}{12} + \frac{3}{4}$ ....

c) $\frac{1}{3} + \frac{3}{4}$ ....

d) $1\frac{2}{5} + 2\frac{2}{3}$ ....

e) $\frac{1}{6} + 4\frac{1}{3}$ ....

f) $1\frac{3}{10} + \frac{2}{5}$ ....

Q5   Evaluate, giving your answer as a fraction in its lowest terms:

a) $\frac{11}{4} - \frac{2}{3}$ ....

b) $10 - \frac{2}{5}$ ....

c) $1\frac{3}{4} - 1\frac{1}{5}$ ....

d) $4\frac{2}{3} - \frac{7}{9}$ ....

e) $3\frac{1}{2} - \frac{2}{3}$ ....

f) $8 - \frac{1}{8}$ ....

More Fraction Problems

Try these questions without a calculator:

Q1   What fraction of 1 hour is:

a) 5 minutes? ....

b) 15 minutes? ....

c) 40 minutes? ....

Q2   If a TV programme lasts 40 minutes, what fraction of the programme is left after:

a) 10 minutes? ....

b) 15 minutes? ....

c) 35 minutes? ....

no calculators!!

Q3   In the fast food café, over all the shifts there are eighteen girls and twelve boys waiting at tables. In the kitchen there are six boys and nine girls. What fraction of the <u>kitchen staff</u> are girls, and what fraction of the <u>employees</u> are boys?

Fraction of kitchen staff who are girls ....

Fraction of employees who are boys ....

Use a calculator for the questions below.

Q4   At a college, two fifths of students are female, and three sevenths of these are part-time. If there are 2100 students altogether, how many:

a)   are <u>female</u> students? ....

b)   are <u>part-time</u> female students? ....

Q5   If I pay my gas bill within seven days, I get a <u>reduction</u> of an eighth of the price. If my bill is £120, how much can I save? ....

Q6   The wage bill at an office is £2400 in total. Fred gets one sixth, Greg gets a fifth of the remainder and Hilary gets what is left. How much money are each of them paid?

Fred ...., Greg ...., Hilary ....

Q7   In the summer three friends ran a car-cleaning service. They divided up the profits at the end of the summer according to the <u>proportion of cars</u> each had cleaned. Ali had washed 200 cars, Brenda had washed 50 and Chay had washed 175. The profits were £1700. How much did each person get?

Ali ...., Brenda ...., Chay ....

This is just like Q6, except you've got to work out the fractions of the money they get yourself.

Don't get put off by all the padding in the questions — you've just got to pick out the important stuff.

Fractions, Decimals, %

Q1   Change these fractions to decimals:

a) $\frac{1}{2}$ ....

b) $\frac{3}{4}$ ....

c) $\frac{7}{10}$ ....

d) $\frac{19}{20}$ ....

e) $\frac{1}{100}$ ....

f) $\frac{3}{8}$ ....

g) $\frac{2}{1000}$ ....

h) $\frac{1}{3}$ ....

Q2   Change these fractions to percentages:

a) $\frac{1}{4}$ ....

b) $\frac{3}{10}$ ....

c) $\frac{4}{5}$ ....

d) $\frac{12}{25}$ ....

e) $\frac{8}{100}$ ....

f) $\frac{2}{40}$ ....

g) $\frac{7}{8}$ ....

h) $\frac{11}{30}$ ....

Q3   Change these decimals to percentages:

a) 0.62 ....

b) 0.74 ....

c) 0.4 ....

d) 0.9 ....

e) 0.07 ....

f) 0.02 ....

g) 0.125 ....

h) 0.987 ....

Q4   Change these percentages to decimals:

a) 25% ....

b) 49% ....

c) 3% ....

d) 30% ....

Q5   Change these percentages to fractions (in their lowest terms):

a) 75% ....

b) 60% ....

c) 15% ....

d) 53% ....

Q6   Change these decimals to fractions (in their lowest terms):

a) 0.5 ....

b) 0.8 ....

c) 0.19 ....

d) 0.25 ....

e) 0.64 ....

f) 0.06 ....

g) 0.125 ....

h) 0.075 ....

A FRACTION IS A DECIMAL IS A PERCENTAGE —
they're all just different ways of saying "a bit of" something.

Percentages

Finding "something %" of "something-else" is really
quite simple — so you'd better be sure you know how.

1) "OF" means "×".
2) "PER CENT" means "OUT OF 100".

Example: 30% of 150 would be
translated as $\dfrac{30}{100} \times 150 = 45$.

Q1 Try these <u>without</u> a calculator:

a) 50% of £12 = ...

b) 25% of £20 = ...

c) 10% of £50 ....

d) 5% of £50 = ...

e) 30% of £50 = ...

f) 75% of £80 = ...

g) 10% of 90 cm = ...

h) 10% of 4.39 kg = ...

Now you can use a calculator:

i) 8% of £16 = ...

j) 85% of 740 kg = ...

k) 40% of 40 minutes = ...

A school has 750 pupils.

l) If 56% of the pupils are boys, what percentage are girls? ....

m) How many boys are there in the school? ....

n) One day, 6% of the pupils were absent. How many pupils was this? ....

o) 54% of the pupils have a school lunch, 38% bring sandwiches and the rest go home for
lunch. How many pupils go home for lunch?

....

Q2 VAT (value added tax) is charged at a rate of 17.5% on many goods and services.
Complete the table showing how much VAT has to be paid and the new price of each
article.

Article	Basic price	VAT at 17.5%	Price + VAT
Tin of paint	£6.75		
Paint brush	£3.60		
Sand paper	£1.55		

Percentages

Q3 John bought a new PC. The tag in the shop said it cost £890 + VAT.
If VAT is charged at 17½%, how much did he pay?

....

Q4 Admission to Wonder World is £18 for adults. A child ticket is 60% of the adult price.

a) How much will it cost for one adult and 4 children to enter Wonder World?

....

b) How much will two adults and three children spend on entrance tickets?

....

Q5 Daphne earns an annual wage of £18900. She doesn't pay tax on the first £3400 that she earns. How much income tax does she pay when the rate of tax is:

a) 25% ? ....   **b)** 40% ? ....

Q6 Terence paid £4700 for his new motorcycle. Each year its value decreased by 12%.

a) How much was it worth when it was one year old? ....

b) How much was it worth when it was two years old? ....

Q7 A double-glazing salesman is paid 10% commission on every sale he makes.
In addition he is paid a £50 bonus if the sale is over £500.

a) If a customer buys £499 worth from the salesman, what is his commission?

....

b) How much extra will he earn if he persuades the customer in **a)** to spend an extra £20?

....

c) How much does he earn if he sells £820 worth of windows?

....

Q8

Bed & breakfast £37 per person. Evening meal £15 per person

2 people stay at The Pickled Parrot for 2 nights and have an evening meal each night. How much is the total cost, if VAT is added at 17½% ?

....

Percentages

Divide the new amount by the old, then × 100... or if you've been practising on your calc, you'll know you can just press the % button for the 2nd bit...

Q9 Express each of the following as a percentage. Round off if necessary.

a) £6 of £12 = ...

b) £4 of £16 = ...

c) 600 kg of 750 kg = ...

d) 6 hours of one day = ...

e) 1 month of a year = ...

f) 25 m of 65 m = ...

Q10 Calculate the percentage saving of the following:

eg. Trainers: Was £72 Now £56 Saved ..£16.. of £72 = ...22...%

a) Jeans: Was £45 Now £35 Saved .... of £45 = ...%

b) CD: Was £14.99 Now £12.99 Saved .... of .... = ...%

c) Shirt: Was £27.50 Now £22.75 Saved .... of .... = ...%

d) TV: Was £695 Now £435 Saved .... = ...%

e) Microwave: Was £132 Now £99 Saved .... = ...%

Q11 a) If Tim Hangman won 3 out of the 5 sets in the Wimbledon Men's Final, what percentage of the sets did he not win?

....%

b) Of Ibiza's 25,000 tourists last Summer, 23,750 were between 16 and 30 years old. What percentage of the tourists were not in this age group?

....%

c) Jeff went on a diet. At the start he weighed 92 kg, after one month he weighed 84 kg. What is his percentage weight loss?

....%

d) In their first game of the season, Nowcastle had 24,567 fans watching the game. By the final game there were 32,741 fans watching. What is the percentage increase in the number of fans?

....%

Regular Polygons

Regular polygons are just shapes that follow certain rules — which makes them ideal exam question material...

Q1 Describe what a regular polygon is.

....

....

Q2 What are the names given to the two types of angles associated with regular polygons?

....

Q3 Sketch a regular hexagon and draw in all its lines of symmetry.
State the order of rotational symmetry.

Rotational symmetry is just the number of positions in which the shape looks the same.

Order of rotational symmetry is ....

Q4 Complete the following table:

Name	Sides	Lines of Symmetry	Order of Rotational Symmetry
Equilateral Triangle			
Square		4	
Regular Pentagon			
Regular Hexagon	6		
Regular Heptagon	7		
Regular Octagon			8
Regular Decagon	10		

32

Regular Polygons

You need to remember these two formulas for polygons:

Sum of Exterior angles = 360°

and **Sum of Interior angles = (n – 2) × 180°**

(n is the number of sides)

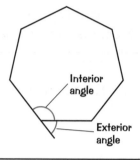

Interior angle

Exterior angle

Q5 Here is a regular octagon:

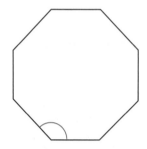

a) What is the total of its eight interior angles? ....

b) What is the size of the marked angle? ....

Here is a regular pentagon:

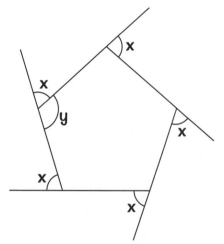

c) The five angles marked x are its exterior angles. What do they add up to?

....

d) Work out the value of x.

....

e) Use your answer from part **d)** to work out the value of angle y.

....

Q6 The diagram shows a regular hexagon:

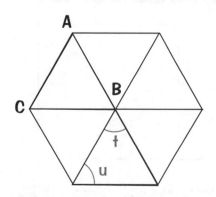

a) Work out the size of angles t and u.

....

b) What type of triangle is ABC? ....

Symmetry

To work out if you've got a line of symmetry, just imagine you're folding the shape in half. If the sides will fold exactly together, then hey presto, it's symmetrical about the fold.

Q1 These shapes have more than one line of symmetry.
Draw the lines of symmetry using dotted lines.

a)

b)

c)

Q2 Some of the letters of the alphabet have lines of symmetry.
Draw the lines of symmetry using dotted lines.

A B C D E F G H I J K L M

N O P Q R S T U V W X Y Z

Q3 Write down the order of rotational symmetry of each of the following shapes:

a)

square

b)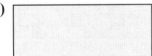

rectangle

c)

equilateral triangle

d)

parallelogram

Q4 Complete the following diagrams so that they have rotational symmetry about centre C of the order stated:

a) order 2

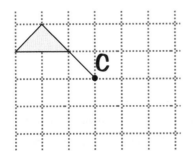

b) order 4

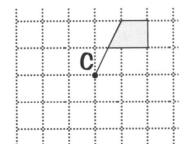

c) order 3

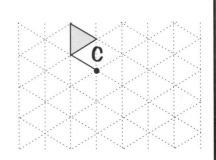

Symmetry

Q5 Which of the following shaded planes are planes of symmetry?

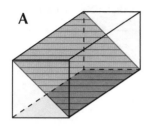

A

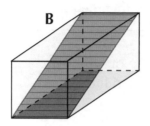

B

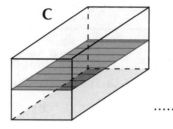

C

....

Q6 Give 6 examples of a plane of symmetry for a cube:
(The first one is done for you)

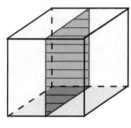

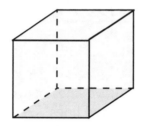

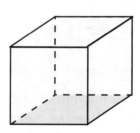

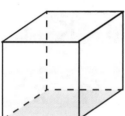

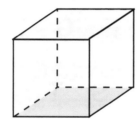

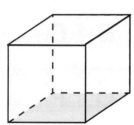

Q7 A tessellation is a pattern made with identical 2-D shapes which fit together exactly leaving no gaps. Continue these tessellations.

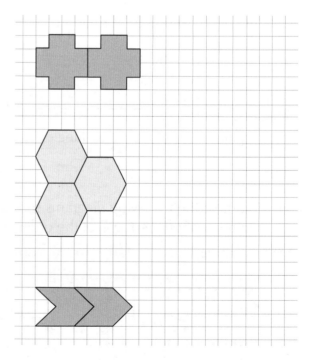

SECTION TWO — SHAPES AND AREA

Quadrilaterals

Here's a few easy marks for you — all you've got to do is remember the shapes and a few facts about them... it's a waste of marks not to bother.

Fill in the blanks in the table.

NAME	DRAWING	DESCRIPTION
Square		Sides of equal length. Opposite sides parallel. Four right angles.
....	....	Opposite sides parallel and the same length. Four right angles.
....		Opposite sides are .... and equal. Opposite angles are equal.
Trapezium		Only .... sides are parallel.
Rhombus		A parallelogram but with all sides ....
Kite	....	Two pairs of adjacent equal sides.

Families of Triangle

Q1 Fill in the gaps in these sentences.

a) An isosceles triangle has .... equal sides and .... equal angles.

b) A triangle with all its sides equal and all its angles equal is called an

.... triangle.

c) A scalene triangle has .... equal sides and .... equal angles.

d) A triangle with one right-angle is called a .... triangle.

Q2 By joining dots draw four different isosceles triangles — one in each box.

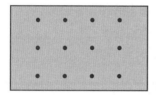 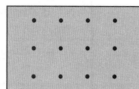 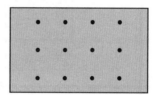 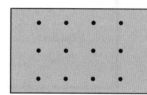

Q3 Using three different coloured pencils:
Find an equilateral triangle and shade it in.
Using a different colour, shade in two different
right angled triangles.
With your last colour shade in two different
scalene triangles.

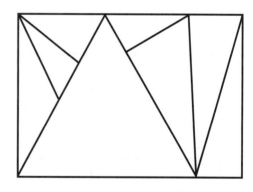

Q4 How many triangles are there in this diagram?

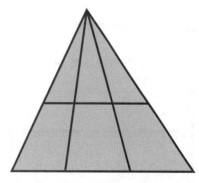

....

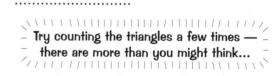
Try counting the triangles a few times —
there are more than you might think...

What sort of triangles are they?

....

There are only 4 types of triangle, so make sure you know them all —
think of all those nice fat juicy marks...

Vertices, Faces and Edges

Q1 What are the names of these shapes?

a)

....

b)

....

c)

....

Q2 Fill in the boxes in the table.

> **Vertex just means corner.**

	Name of SHAPE	number of FACES	number of EDGES	number of VERTICES
cube				
cuboid				
triangular prism				
square-based pyramid				

Name that shape... they're really keen on putting these in the Exam —
gonna have to get learning those shape names, aren't you...

Perimeters

What you've gotta do with these is add up all the sides to get the perimeter.
If there's no drawing, do one yourself — then you won't forget any of the sides.

Q1   Work out the perimeters of the following shapes :

a)

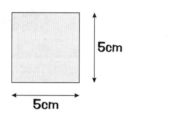

Square Perimeter = ... cm

b)

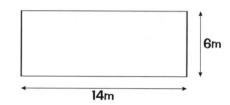

Rectangle Perimeter =

= (2 × ......) + (2 × ......) = ... m

c)

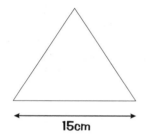

Equilateral Triangle

Perimeter = 3 × ...... = ... cm

d)

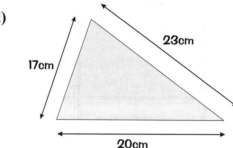

Triangle

Perimeter = ... + ... + ...

= .... cm

e)

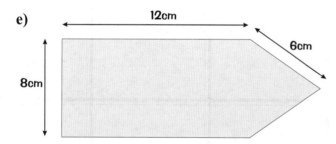

Symmetrical Five Sided Shape

Perimeter = ... + ... + ... + ... + ...

= .... cm

f)

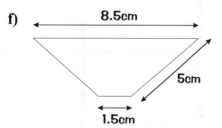

Symmetrical Four Sided Shape

Perimeter = ... + ... + ... + ... = ... cm

Q2 a) A square garden has sides of length 10 m.
How much fencing is needed to go around it?   .... m.

b) A photo measures 17.5 cm by 12.5 cm.
What is the total length of the frame around it?   .... cm.

Perimeters

Q3   Find the perimeter of these shapes (you may need to work out some of the lengths):

a)

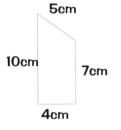

Perimeter ....

b)

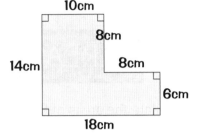

Perimeter ....

c)

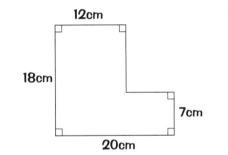

Perimeter ....

d)

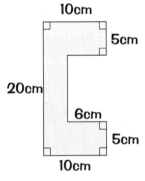

Perimeter ....

e)

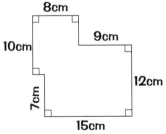

Perimeter ....

f)

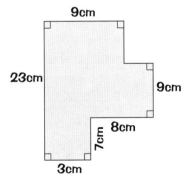

Perimeter ....

Areas of Rectangles

For rectangles and squares, working out the area is a piece
of pie — it's just **LENGTH TIMES WIDTH**. Nowt more to it.

AREA = LENGTH × WIDTH

Q1   Calculate the areas of the following rectangles:

a) Length = 10 cm, Width = 4 cm,   Area = ... × ..... = ... cm².

b) Length = 55 cm, Width = 19 cm, Area = ... cm².

c) Length = 12 m,   Width = 7 m,   Area = ... m².

d) Length = 155 m, Width = 28 m,   Area = ... m².

e) Length = 3.7 km, Width = 1.5 km, Area = ... km².

Q2   Measure the lengths and widths of each of these rectangles, then calculate the area.

a)

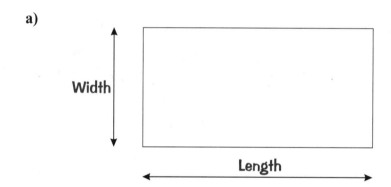

Width = ... cm

Length = ... cm

Area = ... cm²

b)

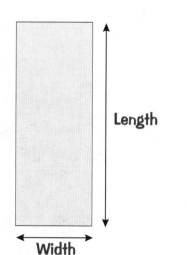

Width = ... cm

Length = ... cm

Area = ... cm²

Areas of Triangles

Triangles aren't much different, but <u>remember</u> to **TIMES BY THE ½.**

Area = ½ (Base × Height)

Q1 Calculate the areas of the following triangles:

a) Base = 12 cm, Height = 9 cm,   Area = $\frac{1}{2}$ (...... × ......) = ... cm².

b) Base = 5 cm, Height = 3 cm,   Area = ... cm².

c) Base = 25 m, Height = 7 m,   Area = ... m².

d) Base = 1.6 m, Height = 6.4 m,   Area = ... m².

e) Base = 700 cm, Height = 350 cm,   Area = ... cm².

Q2 Measure the base and height of each of these triangles, then calculate the area.

a)

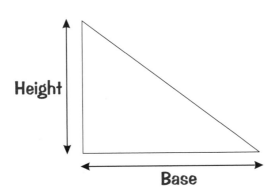

Height = ... cm

Base = ... cm

Area = ... cm²

b)

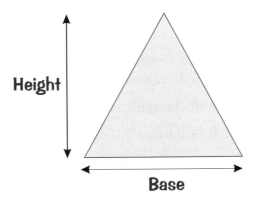

Height = ... cm

Base = ... cm

Area = ... cm²

Composite Areas

Bit more tricky, these... but look — they're all just rectangles and triangles.
Work out each bit separately, then add the areas together — easy.

Calculate the areas of these composite shapes...

Q1

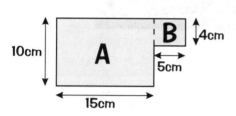

Shape A: length = ... width = ...

Area = ... × .... = ... cm²

Shape B: length = ... width = ...

Area = ... × .... = ... cm²

Total (area A + area B) = ... + ... = ... cm²

Q2 Shape A (rectangle): .... × .... = ... cm²

Shape B (triangle): ½ (base x height)

Base = ... cm , Height = ... cm

Area = ½ (........ × ....) = ... cm²

Total Area = ... + ... = ... cm²

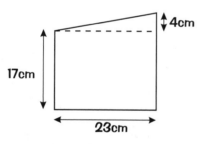

Q3

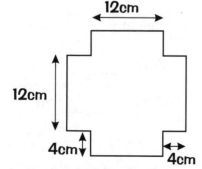

Shape A (rectangle): .... × .... = ... cm²

Shape B (triangle): ½ (........ × ....) = ... cm²

Total Area = ... + ... = ... cm²

Q4 Draw a dotted line to divide this shape.

Shape A (rectangle): .... × .... = ... cm²

Shape B (triangle): ½(........ × ....) = ... cm²

Total Area = ... + ... = ... cm²

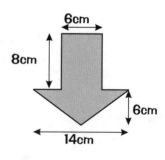

Q5

Draw dotted lines to divide this shape.

Shape A (rectangle): .... × .... = ... cm²

Shape B (square): .... × .... = ... cm²

Total Area = (4 × Shape A) + Shape B = ... cm²

More Areas

Q1 This parallelogram has an area of 4773 mm².
How long is its base?

....

....

43 mm

base

\\\ \ \\ \\\\\\\\\\\\\\\\\\\\/ \\\\\\\\ / / / / / /,
Remember, a parallelogram is just a sloping
rectangle — so area = base × vertical height.
/ / / / / \\\\\\\\\\\\\\\\\\\\\\\\ \ \\\\

Q2 A simple tent is to be made in the shape of a triangular prism.
The dimensions are shown in the diagram.

a) The two end faces are isosceles triangles.
Find their areas.

....

....

3.2 m

3.4 m

2.3 m

4 m

b) The two sides are rectangles. Find their areas.

....

c) The groundsheet is also a rectangle. Find its area.

....

d) How much material is required to make this tent?

....

Q3 A lawn is to be made 48 m².
a) If its width is 5 m, how long is it?

....

b) Rolls of turf are 50 cm wide and 11 m long.
How many rolls need to be ordered to grass the lawn?

....

....

\\\ \ | | | | | | | | | | | | / / / / /,
Start by finding the area of 1 roll.
Then work out how many rolls
fit into the area of the lawn.
/ / / | | | | | | | | | | | \ \\\

Circles

 Don't worry about that π bit — it just stands for the number **3.14159...** Sometimes you'll be told to round it off to **3** or **3.14**. If not, just use the π button on your calculator.

Q1 Draw a circle with radius 3 cm.
On your circle label the circumference,
a radius and a diameter.

Q2 Calculate the circumference of these circles.
Take π to be 3.14.

a) 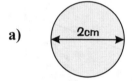 Circumference = π × diameter = ...

b) Circumference = π × diameter = ...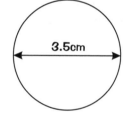

c)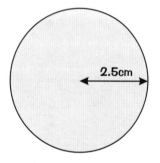

Remember to work out the diameter first.

Diameter = radius × 2 = ...

Circumference = ...

d) A circle of radius 3.5 cm. ....

Q3 A coin has a diameter of 1.7 cm. What is its circumference?

....

Q4 A plant is in a pot. The radius of the top of the pot is 4.5 cm.
Calculate the circumference of the top of the pot.

....

Q5 The circumference of a circle is 195 cm.
Calculate its diameter correct to 3 sig. figs.

Diameter = ...

Circles

Q6 Calculate the area of each circle.
Write your answers to **a)** and **b)** as multiples of π.

a)

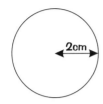

Area = π × radius² = ...

b) A circle of radius 9 cm.   Area = π × radius² = ...

Give your answers to **c)** and **d)** to 3 sig. figs.

c)

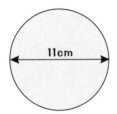

You must find the radius first.

Radius = diameter / 2 = ...

Area = ...

d) A circle of diameter 28 cm. Radius = ...

Area = ...

Q7 Find the area of one face of a 10p coin, radius 1.2 cm.
Give your answer correct to 3 sig. figs.

Area = ...

Q8 A circular table has a diameter of 50 cm.
Find the area of the table to 3 sig. figs.

Area = ...

Q9 What is the area of this semicircular rug?
Give your answer to the nearest whole number.

Area = ...

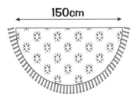

Q10 This circular pond has a circular path around it. The radius of the pond is 72 m and the
path is 2 m wide. Calculate to the nearest whole number:

the area of the pond ....

the area of the path ....

Volume

Q1 Each shape has been made from centimetre cubes. The volume of a centimetre cube is 1 cubic cm. How many cubes are there in each shape? What is the volume of each shape?

a)

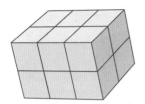

There are ...... cubes.
The volume is
...... cubic cm.

b)

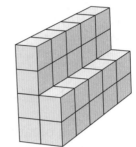

There are ...... cubes.
The volume is
...... cubic cm.

c)

There are ...... cubes.
The volume is
...... cubic cm.

d)

There are ...... cubes.
The volume is
...... cubic cm.

e)

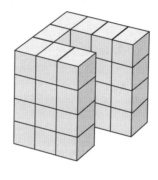

There are ...... cubes.
The volume is
...... cubic cm.

f)

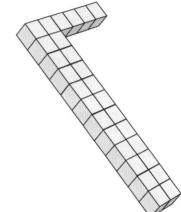

There are ...... cubes.
The volume is
...... cubic cm.

g)

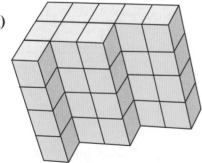

There are ...... cubes.
The volume is ...... cubic cm.

h)

There are ...... cubes.
The volume is ...... cubic cm.

**You simply add up the cubes... but make sure you don't miss any —
remember that there are some rows at the back too.**

Volume

Finding volumes of cubes and cuboids is just like finding areas of squares and rectangles — except you've got an extra side to multiply by.

Q2   A match box measures 7 cm by 4 cm by 5 cm. What is its volume?

....

Q3   A cereal box measures 30 cm by 6 cm by 15 cm. What is its volume?

....

Q4   A video casette case measures 20 cm by 3 cm by 10 cm.
What is its volume?

....

Q5   A room is 2.5 m tall, 8 m long and 5 m wide. What is its volume?

....

Q6   Which holds more, a box measuring 12 cm by 5 cm by 8 cm or a box measuring 10 cm by 6 cm by 9 cm?

....

Q7   What is the volume of a cube of side:

a) 5 cm? ....

b) 9 cm? ....

c) 15 cm? ....

Q8   A box measures 9 cm by 5 cm by 8 cm. What is its volume? ....
What is the volume of a box twice as long,
twice as wide and twice as tall?

....

Q9   An ice cube measures 2 cm by 2 cm by 2 cm. What is its volume? ....
Is there enough room in a container measuring
8 cm by 12 cm by 10 cm for 100 ice cubes?

....

Volume

Contrary to popular belief, there isn't anything that complicated about prisms — they're only solids with the same shape all the way through. The only bit that sometimes takes a bit longer is finding the cross-sectional area. (Back a few pages for a reminder of areas.)

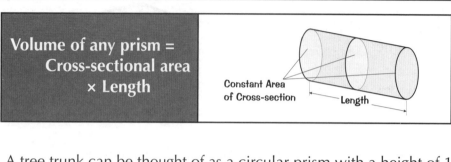

Volume of any prism = Cross-sectional area × Length

Constant Area of Cross-section — Length

Q10 A tree trunk can be thought of as a circular prism with a height of 1.7 m. If the trunk has diameter 60 cm what volume of wood is this in m³?

....

Q11 A coffee mug is a cylinder closed at one end. The internal radius is 7 cm and the internal height is 9 cm.

a) Taking π to be 3.14, find the volume of liquid the mug can hold.

....

b) If 1200 cm³ of liquid is poured into the mug, find the depth to the nearest whole cm.

....

....

The depth is just the length of mug taken up by the liquid — which you find by rearranging the volume formula.

Q12 An unsharpened pencil can be thought of as a regular hexagonal prism with a cylinder of graphite through the centre.

a) By considering a hexagon to be made up of six equilateral triangles, calculate the area of the cross-section of the hexagonal prism shown.

You need to use a bit of Pythagoras to find the height of the triangles.

....

b) Find the area of wood in the cross-section.

circle 2mm diameter

....

hexagon 4mm each side

c) If the pencil is 20 cm long what is the volume of wood in the pencil?

....

Solids and Nets

Q1   Which of the following nets would make a cube? ....

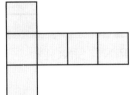

a)

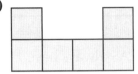

b)

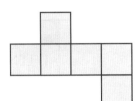

c)

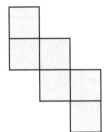

d)

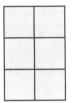

e)

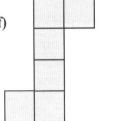

f)

Q2   On a separate piece of paper, draw an accurate net for each of the following solids.

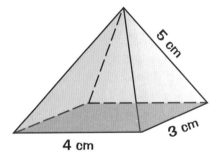

a)

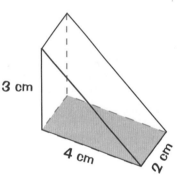

b)

Q3   This net will make a common, mathematical solid. Name the solid:

....

You've got to think about folding the net up to make the shape — if you're struggling, the best thing to do is practise your origami skills...

Length, Area and Volume

 Top tip

Time to get your brain in gear — these can get pretty confusing, believe me.

You need to know these three facts:

1) LENGTH FORMULAS always have LENGTHS OCCURING SINGLY
2) AREA FORMULAS always have lengths MULTIPLIED IN PAIRS
3) VOLUME FORMULAS always have lengths multiplied in GROUPS OF THREE

Q1   p, q and r are lengths. State for each of the following, whether the formula gives a length, an area, a volume or none of these:

a) $p + q$ ....

c) $p^2q^2 + pr^2$ ....

b) $pq - rq$ ....

d) pr/q ....

Q2   w, x, y and z are lengths. State for each of the following, whether the formula gives a length, an area or a volume, when numbers are substituted in for the dummy variables:

a) $\dfrac{xy}{w}$

b) $\dfrac{xy^2 - w^2y}{z^2}$

c) $\dfrac{x^2}{w} + \dfrac{w^2}{y} + \dfrac{y^2}{z} + \dfrac{z^3}{x^2}$

....

Q3   If b and h are lengths, is ½bh an area formula? ....

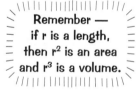

Remember —
if r is a length,
then r^2 is an area
and r^3 is a volume.

Q4   If x and h are lengths, could this be a perimeter formula:

$$x + x + h + h + h?$$ ....

Q5   a, b, and c are lengths, r is the radius, $\pi = 3.14$.
State whether the formula gives a perimeter, area or neither of these.

a) $3\pi r^2 + abc$ ....

c) $17ab + \pi r^2$ ....

b) $6\pi r + a - 6c$ ....

d) $\dfrac{16abc}{8b}$ ....

If you ever see something like r^6 then rub your eyes because it's gone wrong — unless you're an alien from a 6-dimensional universe, in which case you'll feel right at home.

Metric and Imperial Units

You'd better learn ALL these conversions
— you'll be well and truly scuppered without them.

APPROXIMATE CONVERSIONS

1 kg = 2.2 lbs	1 gallon = 4.5 l	1 inch = 2.5 cm
	1 litre = 1.75 pints	5 miles = 8 km

Q1 The table shows the distances in miles between 4 cities in Scotland. Fill in the blank table with the equivalent distances in kilometres.

Aberdeen			
105	Inverness		
150	175	Glasgow	
125	155	45	Edinburgh

Aberdeen			
	Inverness		
		Glasgow	
			Edinburgh

Q2 Change each of these weights from kilograms to pounds.

10 kg = ... lbs   16 kg = ... lbs   75 kg = ... lbs

Change each of these capacities in gallons to litres.

5 galls = ... l   14 galls = ... l   40 galls = ... l

Q3 Convert the measurements of the note book and pencil to centimetres.

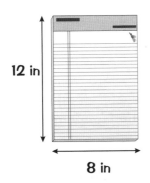

12 in = ... cm

8 in = ... cm

5 in = ... cm

Metric and Imperial Units

Q4 The water butt in my garden holds 20 gallons of rain-water. How many litres is this?

....

Q5 Tom walked 17 km in one day, while Dave walked 10 miles. Who walked further?

....

....

> It doesn't matter which distance you convert — but here it's easier to convert David's miles to km.

Q6 A recipe for a gigantic chocolate cake requires 8 lb of sugar. How many 1 kg bags of sugar does Sarah need to buy so that she can make the cake?

....

Q7 David is throwing a party for himself and 15 of his friends. He decides that it would be nice to make a bowl of fruit punch and carefully follows a recipe for 24 pints worth.

a) How many litres of fruit punch is this?

....

> Read the questions carefully — it's back to pints for part b), then litres again for part c).

b) If divided equally, how many pints of fruit punch is this per person at the party?

....

c) How many litres of fruit punch is this per person at the party?

....

Rounding Off

Q1 Round the following to the nearest whole number:

a) 2.9 ....   b) 26.8 ....   c) 2.24 ....

d) 11.11 ....   e) 6.347 ....   f) 43.5 ....

g) 9.99 ....   h) 0.41 ....

Nearest __whole number__ means you look at the digit after the decimal point to decide whether to round up or down.

Q2 An average family has 2.3 children, how many children is this to the nearest whole number?

....

Q3 By the time she is 25 the average woman will have driven 4.72 cars. What is this to the nearest whole number?

....

Q4 Give these amounts to the nearest pound:

a) £4.29 ....   b) £16.78 ....   c) £12.06 ....

d) £7.52 ....   e) £0.93 ....   f) £14.50 ....

g) £7.49 ....   h) £0.28 ....

Q5 Give these amounts to the nearest hour:

a) 2 hours 12 minutes ....   b) 36 minutes ....

c) 12 hours 12 minutes ....   d) 29 minutes ....

e) 100 minutes ....   f) 90 minutes ....

Rounding Off

Q6   Round off these numbers to the nearest 10:

a) 23 ....   b) 78 ....   c) 65 ....   d) 99 ....

e) 118 ....   f) 243 ....   g) 958 ....   h) 1056 ....

Q7   Round off these numbers to the nearest 100:

a) 627 ....   b) 791 ....   c) 199 ....   d) 450 ....

e) 1288 ....   f) 3329 ....   g) 2993 ....

Q8   Round these off to the nearest 1000:

a) 5200 ....   b) 8860 ....   c) 9870 ....

Q9   Crowd sizes at sports events are often given exactly in newspapers. Round off these exact crowd sizes to the nearest 1000:

a) 23324 ....

b) 36844 ....

c) 49752 ....

Q10   The number of drawing pins in the box has been rounded to the nearest 10.

DRAWING PINS
Contents: 80

What is the least possible number of drawing pins in the box? ....

What is the greatest possible number? ....

Q11   The population of Whichtown is given as 1300 to the nearest 100. What is the smallest number the population could be?

....

What is the largest it could be?

....

When you round numbers off to the nearest unit, the ACTUAL measurement could be up to HALF A UNIT bigger or smaller...

Rounding Off

Q12 Round off these numbers to 1 decimal place (1 d.p.):

a) 7.34 ....   **b)** 8.47 ....   **c)** 12.08 ....   **d)** 28.03 ....

e) 9.35 ....   **f)** 14.618 ....   **g)** 30.409 ....

Q13 Round off the following to 2 d.p.:

a) 17.363 ....   **b)** 38.057 ....   **c)** 0.735 ....

d) 5.99823 ....   **e)** 4.297 ....   **f)** 7.0409 ....

Q14 Now round these to 3 d.p.:

a) 6.3534 ....   **b)** 81.64471 ....   **c)** 0.0075 ....

d) 53.26981 ....   **e)** 754.39962 ....   **f)** 0.000486 ....

Q15 Seven people have a meal in a restaurant. The total bill comes to £60. If they share the bill equally, how much should each of them pay?
Round your answer to 2 d.p.

....

Q16 Round these numbers to 1 significant figure.

a) 12 ....   **b)** 530 ....

c) 1379 ....   **d)** 0.021 ....

e) 1829.62 ....   **f)** 0.296 ....

The 1st significant figure of any number is the first digit which isn't zero.

Q17 At a golf club, a putting green is given as being 500 cm long to 1 significant figure. Give the range of values that the actual length of the green could be.

....

Estimating

Q1 Estimate the answers to these questions…

For example: 12×21 $\underline{10 \times 20 = 200}$

a) 18×12 ……… × ……… = ………

b) 23×21 ……… × ……… = ………

c) 57×46 ……… × ……… = ………

d) 98×145 ……… × ……… = ………

e) $11 \div 4$ ……… ÷ ……… = ………

f) $22 \div 6$ ……… ÷ ……… = ………

g) $97 \div 9$ ……… ÷ ……… = ………

h) $147 \div 14$ ……… ÷ ……… = ………

i) 195×205 ……… × ……… = ………

j) 545×301 ……… × ……… = ………

k) $901 \div 33$ ……… ÷ ……… = ………

l) $1207 \div 598$ ……… ÷ ……… = ………

Q2 Write in the estimates that give the answer shown.

For example: 101×96 $\underline{100 \times 100 = 10000}$

a) 34×19 ……… × ……… = 600

b) 27×32 ……… × ……… = 900

c) 67×89 ……… × ……… = 6300

d) 99×9 ……… × ……… = 1000

e) $56 \div 11$ ……… ÷ ……… = 6

f) $119 \div 17$ ……… ÷ ……… = 6

g) $182 \div 62$ ……… ÷ ……… = 3

h) $317 \div 81$ ……… ÷ ……… = 4

Q3 Andy earns £12,404 a year. Bob earns £58,975 a year. Chris earns £81,006 a year.

a) Estimate how much Andy will earn over 3 years.   £ ………………

b) Estimate how many years Andy will have to work to earn as much as Chris does in one year.   ………………

c) Estimate how much Bob earns per month.   £ ………………

 Round off to NICE EASY CONVENIENT NUMBERS, then use them to do the sum. Easy peasy.

Estimating

Q4 Estimate the following lengths then measure them to see how far out you were:

OBJECT	ESTIMATE	ACTUAL LENGTH
a) Length of your pen or pencil	....	....
b) Width of your thumbnail	....	....
c) Height of this page	....	....
d) Height of the room you are in	....	....

Q5

The ranger is almost 2 m tall. Estimate the height of the giraffe in metres.

....

If you have trouble estimating the height by eye, try measuring the ranger against your finger. Then see how many times that bit of finger fits into the height of the giraffe.

Q6 The distance from A to B is 50 km. Estimate the distance from A to C.

AC = ... km

• A   B •

                              • C

Accuracy and Estimating

Just think casual, technical or scientific...

1) For fairly <u>CASUAL MEASUREMENTS, 2 SIGNIFICANT FIGURES</u> are most appropriate.

Cooking — 250 g (2 sig fig) of sugar, not 253 g (3 SF) or 300 g (1 SF)

2) For <u>IMPORTANT OR TECHNICAL THINGS, 3 SIGNIFICANT FIGURES</u> are essential.

A length that will be cut to fit, eg you'd measure a shelf as 25.6 cm long, not 26 cm or 25.63 cm.

3) Only for <u>REALLY SCIENTIFIC WORK</u> would you need over <u>3 SIGNIFICANT FIGURES</u>.

Only someone really keen would want to know the length of a piece of
string to the nearest tenth of a millimetre — like 34.46 cm, for example.

Q1   A village green is roughly rectangular with a length of 33 m 48 cm and is 24 m and
13 cm wide. Calculate the area of the green in m² to:

a) 2 decimal places ....

b) 3 significant figures   ....

c) State which of parts **a)** and **b)** would be the more reasonable value to use. ....

Q2   Decide on an appropriate degree of accuracy for the following:

a) the total dry weight, 80872 kg, of the space shuttle
OV-102 Columbia with its 3 main engines   ....

b) the distance of 3.872 miles from Mel's house to Bryan's house   ....

c) 1.563 m of fabric required to make a bedroom curtain   ....

d) 152.016 kg of coal delivered to Jeff's house   ....

e) 6 buses owned by the Partridge Flight Bus Company   ....

f) the maximum night temperature of 11.721° forecast
for Birmingham by a TV weather presenter.   ....

Q3   Calculate, giving your answer to an appropriate degree of accuracy:

a) $\dfrac{41.75 \times 0.9784}{22.3 \times 2.54}$ = ...

b) $\dfrac{12.54 + 7.33}{12.54 - 7.22}$ = ...

Conversion Graphs

Q1 This graph can be used to convert the distance (miles) travelled in a taxi to the fare payable (£). How much will the fare be if you travel:

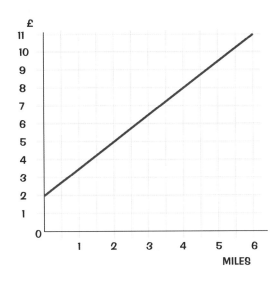

a) 2 miles ....

b) 5 miles ....

c) 10 miles ....

How far would you travel if you paid:

d) £5 ....

e) £11 ....

f) £14 ....

Q2 80 km is roughly equal to 50 miles. Use this information to draw a conversion graph on the grid. Use the graph to estimate the number of miles equal to:

When you've got to draw your own conversion graph, your best bet is to work out a few different values, and mark them on the graph first.

a) 20 km ....

b) 70 km ....

c) 90 km ....

Q3 How many km are equal to:

a) 40 miles ....

b) 10 miles ....

c) 30 miles ....

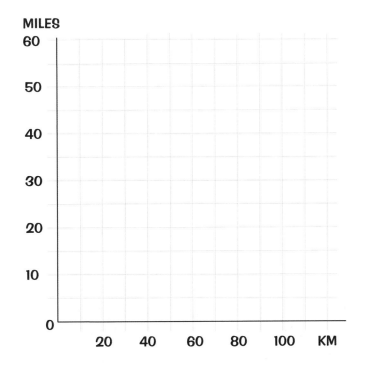

Conversion Factors

The method for these questions is very easy so you might as well learn it...

> 1) Find the **Conversion Factor**
> 2) **Multiply by it AND divide by it**
> 3) Choose the **common sense answer**

The conversion factor is the link between the two units — e.g. there are 100 cm in a m so the conversion factor is 100.

Q1 Fill in the gaps using the conversion factors:

20 mm = ... cm   82 mm = ... cm   .... mm = 6 cm

142 cm = ... m   .... cm = 2.5 m   2550 mm = ... m

9000 m = ... km   3470 m = ... km   .... m = 2 km

3 km = ... cm   .... mm = 3.4 m   .... cm = 0.5 km

6200 mg = ... g   8550 g = ... kg   2.3 kg = ... g

12 000 000 mg = ... kg   1.2 l = ... ml   4400 ml = ... l

Q2 Cashbags Bank are offering the following exchange rates:

> 18 Mexican Pesos to £1 Sterling.
> 200 Japanese Yen to £1 Sterling.
> 2 Canadian Dollars to £1 Sterling.

Use these exchange rates to calculate to the nearest penny the Sterling equivalent of:

a) 200 Mexican Pesos

....

b) 765 Japanese Yen

....

c) 73 Canadian Dollars

....

Using the same exchange rates, convert the following into Canadian Dollars:

d) £56

....

e) 1000 Japanese Yen

....

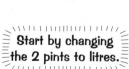

Q3 1 pint = 0.5714 litres. Which is better value, 2 pints of orange juice for £1.20 or 1 litre of orange juice for 95p?

Start by changing the 2 pints to litres.

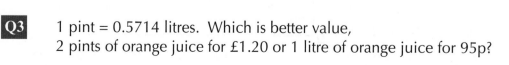

....

SECTION THREE — MEASUREMENTS

Clock Time Questions

I'm sure you know the difference between 12 and 24 hour clocks, but just so there's no excuses...

Q1 The times below are given using the 24 hour system. Using am or pm, give the equivalent time for a 12 hour clock.

a) 0400 ....

c) 0215 ....

e) 2130 ....

b) 1712 ....

d) 1522 ....

f) 0001 ....

Q2 The times below are taken from a 12 hour clock. Give the equivalent 24 hour readings.

a) 10.30 pm ....

c) 12.30 am ....

e) 9.15 am ....

b) 11.22 am ....

d) 12.30 pm ....

f) 3.33 pm ....

Q3 Convert the following into hours and minutes

a) 3.75 hours ....

b) 0.2 hours ....

c) 5.8 hours ....

Q4 This timetable refers to three trains that travel from Asham to Derton.

a) Which train is quickest from Asham to Derton? ....

b) Which train is quickest from Cottingham to Derton?

....

c) I live in Bordhouse. It takes me 8 minutes to walk to the train station. At what time must I leave the house by to arrive in Derton before 2.30 pm?

Asham – Derton			
	Train 1	Train 2	Train 3
Asham	0832	1135	1336
Bordhouse	0914	1216	1414
Cottingham	1002	1259	1456
Derton	1101	1404	1602

....

SECTION THREE — MEASUREMENTS

Compass Directions

Q1

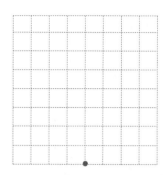

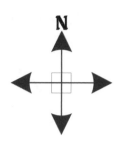

Start at the dot in the middle of the bottom line
and follow the directions. What shape have you drawn? ....

a) West 4 squares.

b) North 4 squares.

c) East 4 squares.

d) South 4 squares.

e) North East through 2 squares.

f) North 4 squares.

g) South West through 2 squares.

h) West 4 squares.

i) North East through 2 squares.

j) East 4 squares.

Q2

Joe's house

Shop

Church

Sue's house

Park

Jane's house

a) What direction does Jane go to get to Sue's house? ....

b) What direction is the church from Joe's house? ....

c) What is South East of Sue's house? ....

d) What is West of Sue's house? ....

e) Jane is at home. She is going to meet Sue in the park. They are going to the shop and
then to Joe's house. Write down Jane's directions.

....

You could use "<u>Never Eat Shredded Wheat</u>" but it's more fun to make one up
— like <u>Not Everyone Squeezes Wombats</u>, or <u>Nine Elves Storm Wales</u>... (hmm)

SECTION THREE — MEASUREMENTS

Three Figure Bearings

Bearings always have three digits — even the small ones...
in other words, if you've measured 60°, you've got to write it as 060°.

This is a map of part of a coastline. The scale is one cm to one km.

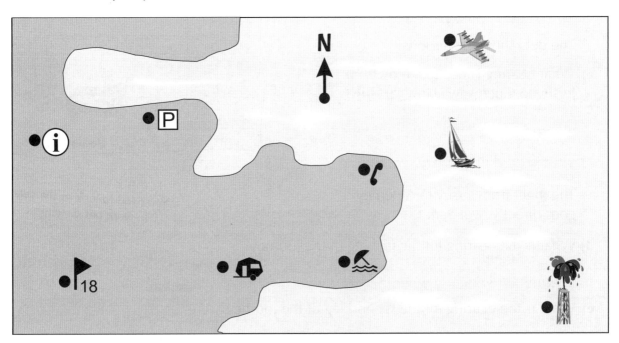

Q1 What is the bearing of the 🚐 from the ⓘ? ....

Q2 What is the bearing of the P from the 🏊? ....

Q3 How far and on what bearing is:

a) The boat from the plane? ....

b) The boat from the oil rig? ....

c) The plane from the oil rig? ....

Q4 The water ski centre is on a bearing of 050° from the golf course, 🏁₁₈, and at a distance of 4.5 km. Put a ☆ where the water ski centre is.

> Do the direction bit first — and draw a straight line. Then measure the correct distance along it.

Q5 There is a lighthouse on the coast. It is at a bearing of 300° from the oil rig and a bearing of 270° from the boat. Mark its position with a △.

64

Three Figure Bearings

Q6 This is a map of the Channel Islands.

a) Which island is furthest West?

....

b) Which island is due East of Guernsey?

....

The dots show the airports.

c) What bearing is needed to fly from Jersey to Guernsey? How far is it?

....

....

You need to look at the scale to work out distances.

The flight from Jersey to Alderney goes directly over Sark.

d) What is the bearing for the first leg of the journey?

....

e) What is the bearing for the second leg of the journey?

....

f) Calculate the total distance flown from Jersey to Alderney.

....

Q7 Mr Brown is standing on the riverbank watching a cricket match on the other side. The bowler is on a bearing of 210° from Mr Brown and the batsman 190° from Mr Brown. When the batsman looks at the bowler he is looking along a bearing of 310°.

a) Draw a rough sketch to show this and put in all the angles given.

Start off by marking Mr Brown on the sketch, then measure the angles one by one.

b) Calculate the bearing of the batsman from the bowler.

....

c) Calculate the bearing of Mr Brown from the batsman.

....

Scale Drawings

Q1 The scale on this map is 1 cm : 4 km.

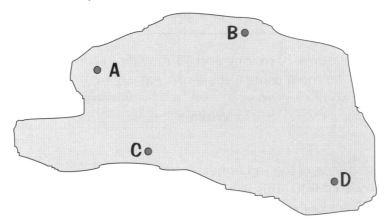

a) Measure the distance from A to B in cm. ....

b) What is the actual distance from A to B in km? ....

c) A helicopter flies on a direct route from A to B, B to C and C to D.
What is the total distance flown in km?

....

Q2 Here is a plan of a garden drawn to a scale of 1 : 50.

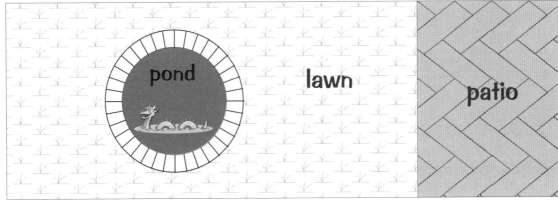

a) Measure the full length of the garden in mm: ....

b) What is the actual length of the garden in mm? ....

c) What is the actual length of the garden in metres? ....

If the scale doesn't say what units it's in, it just means that both sides of the
ratio are the same units — so <u>1 : 1000</u> would mean <u>1 cm : 1000 cm</u>.

Scale Drawings

Watch out for those units... there's quite a mixture here —
you'll have to convert some of them before you can go anywhere.

Q3 A rectangular room measures 20 m long and 15 m wide. Work out the measurements
for a scale drawing of the room using a scale of 1 cm = 2 m.

Length = ... Width = ...

Q4 Katie drew a scale drawing of the top of her
desk. She used a scale of 1:10. This is her
drawing of the computer keyboard. What
are the actual dimensions of it?

Length = ... Width = ...

Q5 This is a scale drawing of Paul's new car.
Measure the length of the car. .... cm.

If the drawing uses a scale of 1 : 90,
work out the actual length of the car.

....

Q6 A rectangular field is 60 m long and 40 m wide. The farmer needs to make a scale
drawing of it. He uses a scale of 1 : 2000. Work out the measurements for the scale
drawing. (Hint — change the m to cm.)

....

....

Q7 A rectangular room is 4.8 m long and 3.6 m wide. Make a scale drawing of it using
a scale of 1 cm to 120 cm. First work out the measurements for the scale drawing.

Length = ...

Width = ...

On your scale drawing mark a window, whose
actual length is 2.4 m, on one long wall and mark
a door, actual width 90 cm, on one short wall.

Window = ...

Door = ...

Formula Triangles

You can use a formula triangle for **ANY FORMULA** with
THREE THINGS, where two are **MULTIPLIED** to give the third.

Eg: area of a rectangle = length × height.
This will give the formula triangle:

**... All you do is cover up what you want with your finger and the other
two bits will tell you how to calculate it. Couldn't be simpler....**

Q1 The formula for finding the area of a triangle is Area = half × base × height, i.e.

$$A = \left(\frac{b}{2}\right) \times h$$

Draw a formula triangle and use it to find:

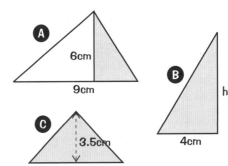

a) the area of triangle A

....

b) the height of triangle B given that its area is 26 cm²

....

c) the base length of triangle C with area 49 cm²

....

Q2 The circumference of a circle is given by the formula c = πd, where c = circumference,
d = diameter. Draw a formula triangle and use it to find:

a) the circumference of a bike wheel with a diameter of 72 cm ....

b) the diameter of a jam jar with a circumference of 21 cm ....

Q3 A formula used by accountants is L = S/Q. L is Lateral Forecast, S is the Spend Parameter
and Q is the Quotient Charter. Draw a formula triangle relating L, S and Q and use it to
find:

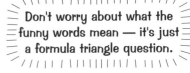
Don't worry about what the
funny words mean — it's just
a formula triangle question.

a) the Lateral Forecast when the Spend Parameter is 120
and the Quotient Charter is 8 ....

b) the Quotient Charter when the Spend Parameter is 408
whilst the Lateral Forecast is 24 ....

Speed

This is an easy enough formula — and of course you can put it in that good old formula triangle as well.

Average speed = $\dfrac{\text{Total distance}}{\text{Total time}}$

Q1   A train travels 240 km in 4 hours. What is its <u>average speed</u>?

....

Q2   A car travels for 3 hours at an average speed of 55 mph. How far has it travelled?

....

Q3   <u>Complete</u> this table.

Distance Travelled	Time taken	Average Speed
210 km	3 hrs	
135 miles		30 mph
	2 hrs 30 mins	42 km/h
9 miles	45 mins	
640 km		800 km/h
	1 hr 10 mins	60 mph

Q4   An athlete can run 100 m in 11 seconds.
Calculate the athlete's speed in:

a) m/s

....

b) km/h

....

Q5   A plane flies over city A at 09.55 and over city B at 10.02.
What is its <u>average</u> speed if these cities are 63 miles apart?

....

Q6   The distance from Kendal (Oxenholme) to London (Euston) is 280 miles. The train travels at an average speed of 63 mph. If I catch the 07.05 from Kendal, can I be at a meeting in London by 10.30? <u>Show all your working</u>.

....

Density

Here we go again — the multi-purpose formula triangle. Learn the positions of M, D and V, plug in the numbers and pull out the answer... magic.

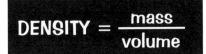

DENSITY = $\dfrac{\text{mass}}{\text{volume}}$

Q1 Find the <u>density</u> of each of these pieces of wood, giving your answer in g/cm³:

a) Mass 3 g, volume 4 cm³

....

b) Mass 20 g, volume 25 cm³

....

c) Mass 12 kg, volume 20,000 cm³

....

d) Mass 14 kg, volume 0.02 m³.

....

Q2 Calculate the <u>mass</u> of each of these objects:

a) a small marble statue of density
2.6 g/cm³ and volume 24 cm³   ....

b) a plastic cube of volume 64 cm³
and density 1.5 g/cm³   ....

c) a gold ingot with density 19.5 g/cm³
measuring 12 cm by 4 cm by 4 cm   ....

d) a pebble with volume 30 cm³
and density 2.5 g/cm³.   ....

Q3 Work out the <u>volume</u> of each of these items:

a) a bag of sugar of mass 1 kg and density 1.6 g/cm³

....

b) a packet of margarine with density 2.8 g/cm³ and mass 250 g

....

c) a 50 kg sack of coal with density 1.8 g/cm³

....

d) a box of cereal with density 0.2 g/cm³ and mass 500 g.

....

Density

Q4 Ice has a density of 0.93 g/cm³.
If the mass of a block of ice is 19.5 kg, what is its <u>volume</u>?

....

Q5 Some petrol in a can has a mass of 4 kg. The density of the petrol is 0.8 g/cm³.
How many litres of petrol are in the can?

....

1 litre = 1000 cm³.

....

Q6 My copper bracelet has a volume of 3.9 cm³. The density of
copper is 8.9 g/cm³. Work out the <u>mass</u> of my bracelet.

....

Q7 A jug holds 1.9 litres of lemonade. The mass of the lemonade is
2 kg. Find the <u>density</u> of the lemonade.

....

Q8 A 1.5 kg bag full of self raising flour measures 12 cm by 18 cm by 6 cm. A 1 kg bag of
granary flour measures 10 cm by 14 cm by 6 cm. Find the <u>density</u> of each sort of flour.

....

....

Estimating Angles

**Estimating angles is easy once you know the 4 special angles —
you can use them as reference points.**

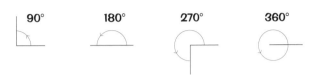

For each of the angles below write down its type, estimate its size (before you
measure it!) and finally measure each angle with a protractor. The first one has
been done for you.

Angle	Type	Estimated Size	Actual Size
a	acute	40°	43°
b			
c			
d			
e			
f			

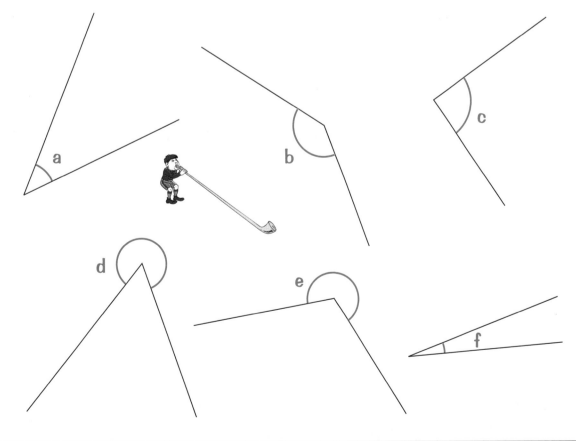

Drawing Angles

These instruments are used to measure angles.

An angle measurer.

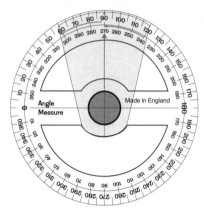

A protractor.

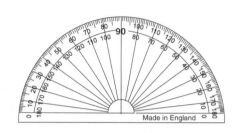

Don't forget protractors have two scales — one going one way and one the other... so make sure you measure from the one that starts with 0°, not 180°.

Q1 Use an angle measurer or protractor to help you to draw the following angles.

a) 20° **b)** 65° **c)** 90°

d) 136° **e)** 225° **f)** 340°

Q2 a) Draw an acute angle and measure it. **b)** Draw an obtuse angle and measure it.

Acute angle measures ....° Obtuse angle measures ....°

c) Draw a reflex angle and measure it.

Reflex angle measures ....°

Angle Rules

Hope you've learnt those angle rules for a straight line and round a point...

Q1 Work out the angles labelled:

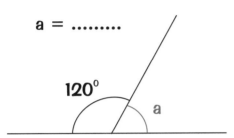

a = ...

120°   a

b = ...

76°   b

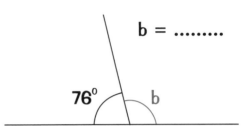

c = ...

c   100°   120°

d = ...

87°   d   118°   125°

e = ...

f = ...

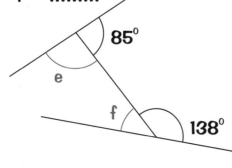

85°   e   f   138°

g = ...

h = ...

i = ...

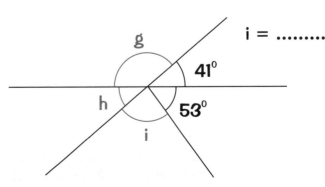

g   41°   h   53°   i

Angle Rules

The three angles inside a triangle always add up to 180°

Q2 Work out the missing angle in each of these triangles. The angles are not drawn to scale so you cannot measure them.

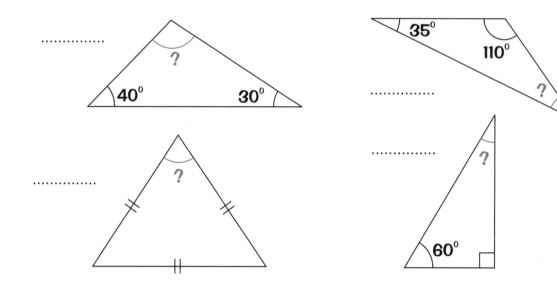

....

40°   30°

35°
110°
....   ?

....   ?

....   ?

60°

The angles in a quadrilateral always add up to 360°

Q3 Work out the missing angles in these quadrilaterals.

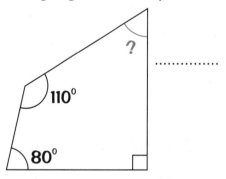

?
....
110°
80°

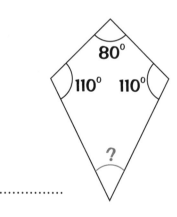

80°
110°   110°
?
....

Q4 Work out the missing angles in these diagrams.

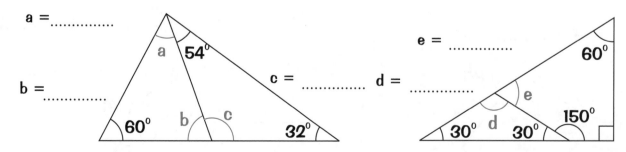

a =..............

b =..............

a   54°

60°   b   c   32°

c = ...   d = ...

e = ...

60°

e

30°   d   30°   150°

You'd better get learning these rules too — they're not that hard, and you'll be well and truly stumped without them.

Three-letter Angle Notation

Three Letter Angle Notation — bit of a mouthful, isn't it...
but it's actually quite easy. Read and enjoy...

Using Three Letters to Specify Angles	
1) The <u>MIDDLE LETTER</u> tells you where the angle is. 2) The <u>OTHER TWO LETTERS</u> tell you which two lines enclose the angle.	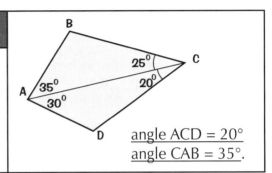 angle ACD = 20° angle CAB = 35°.

Q1 **a)** State, with reasons, angle QRP.

....

b) Calculate angle RPQ.

....

c) What do all the angles sum to at P?

....

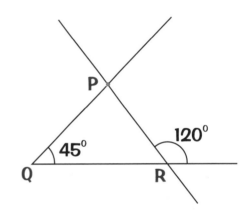

Q2 **a)** Calculate angle XBY. ....

b) Find angle YXB. ....

c) Calculate angle BZY.

....

d) Which angle is equal to BZY?

....

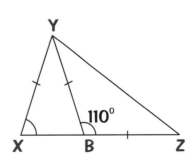

Parallel Lines

Once you know the **3 ANGLE RULES** for parallel lines, you can find all the angles out from just one — ah, such fun...

c = f and d = e — Alternate angles

a = e, c = g, b = f and d = h — Corresponding angles

d + f = 180⁰, c + e = 180⁰ — Supplementary angles

Find the sizes of the angles marked by letters in these diagrams.
Write down what sort of angle each one is.

NOT DRAWN TO SCALE

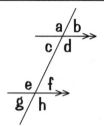

a = ...

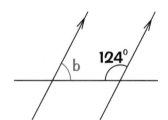

b = ...

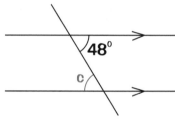

c = ...

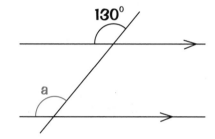

d = ...

e = ...

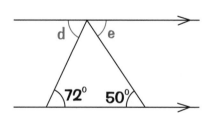

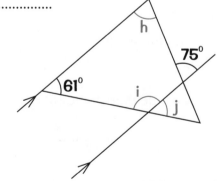

h = ...

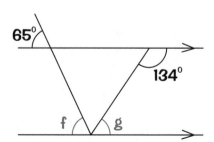

f = ...

g = ...

i = ...

j = ...

SECTION FOUR — ANGLES AND GEOMETRY

Pythagoras' Theorem

If you're as big a fan of Pythagoras as me, you'll ignore him and use this method instead:

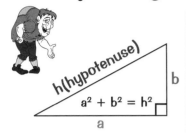

$a^2 + b^2 = h^2$

h(hypotenuse)

b

a

The Simple Three Step Method
1) SQUARE the two numbers that you are given.
2) To find the <u>longest side, ADD</u> the two squared numbers.
To find a <u>shorter side, SUBTRACT</u> the smaller one from the larger.
3) Take the SQUARE ROOT. Then check that your answer is sensible.

Q1 Using Pythagoras' theorem, calculate the length of the third side
in these triangles, giving your answers to <u>3 significant figures</u>.

$c^2 =$ .... $+$ .... $=$ ...., $c =$ ....

$d^2 =$ .... $+$ .... $=$ ...., $d =$ ....

$e^2 =$ .... $-$ .... $=$ ...., $e =$ ....

$f^2 =$ .... $-$ .... $=$ ...., $f =$ ....

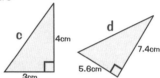

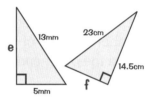

Q2 Using Pythagoras' theorem, work out which of these triangles have right-angles.

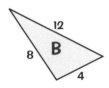

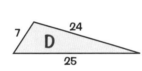

If they don't have right-angles, the numbers won't fit the formula.

....

....

Q3 Calculate the missing lengths in these quadrilaterals. Give your answers to 3 sig. figs.

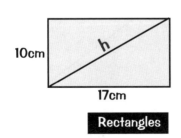

Rectangles

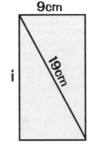

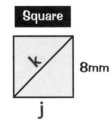

Square

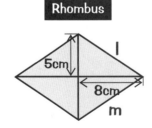

Rhombus

h = ..., i = ...,

j = ..., k = ...,

l = ..., m = ...

Loci and Constructions

You've gotta be ultra neat with these — you'll lose easy marks if your pictures are scruffy — and let's face it, you'd rather have them, wouldn't you.

Constructions should always be done as accurately as possible using:

sharp pencil, ruler, compasses, protractor (set-square).

Q1 a) Draw a circle with radius 4 cm.

Draw in a diameter of the circle. Label one end of the diameter X and the other end Y.

Mark a point somewhere on the circumference — not too close to X or Y. Label your point T. Join X to T and T to Y.

Measure angle XTY.

Angle XTY = ...°

b) Make an accurate drawing below of the triangle on the right. Measure side AB on your triangle, giving your answer in millimetres.

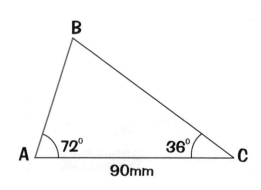

AB = ... mm

Loci and Constructions

Work through these questions bit by bit, and remember the following...

LOCUS — a line showing all points obeying the given rule.
BISECTOR — a line splitting an angle or line exactly in two.

Q2 **a)** In the space to the left, construct a triangle ABC with AB = 4 cm, BC = 5 cm, AC = 3 cm.

b) Construct the perpendicular bisector of AB and where this line meets BC, label the new point D.

Q3

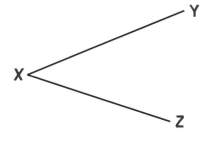

The diagram on the left shows two lines XY and XZ which meet at the point X. Construct the angle bisector of YXZ.

Q4 On a plain piece of paper mark two points A and B which are 6 cm apart.

a) Draw the locus of points which are 4 cm from A.

b) Draw the locus of points which are 3 cm from B.

c) There are 2 points which are both 4 cm from A and 3 cm from B. Label them X and Y.

Loci and Constructions

Q5 Two churches with bell towers are 2 km apart. On a still day, the sound of the bells can be heard 1.5 km away. To the right, draw an accurate diagram to show the two churches, and for each one, draw the locus of points where its bell can be heard. Shade the area where <u>both</u> bells can be heard.

Q6 Tony likes to look at the tree in his garden. The diagram to the right shows the position of the tree relative to his bedroom window. Tony wants to position his bed in such a way that he can see the tree in the morning as he awakes.

Carefully <u>shade</u> on the diagram the area in which Tony could position his bed.

He doesn't need to be able to see the whole tree.

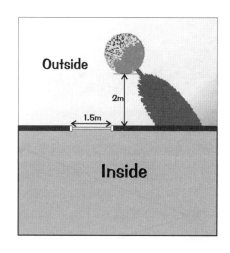

Q7 With the aid of a pair of compasses accurately draw an equilateral triangle with sides 5 cm. Now accurately draw a square with sides 6 cm.

Congruence

I reckon these are pretty easy — so while you're racing through them, you can be thinking: "**3** shapes are **CONGRUENT** (<u>exactly the same</u>) and **1** isn't."

In each of the following sets of shapes underline the one which is not congruent.

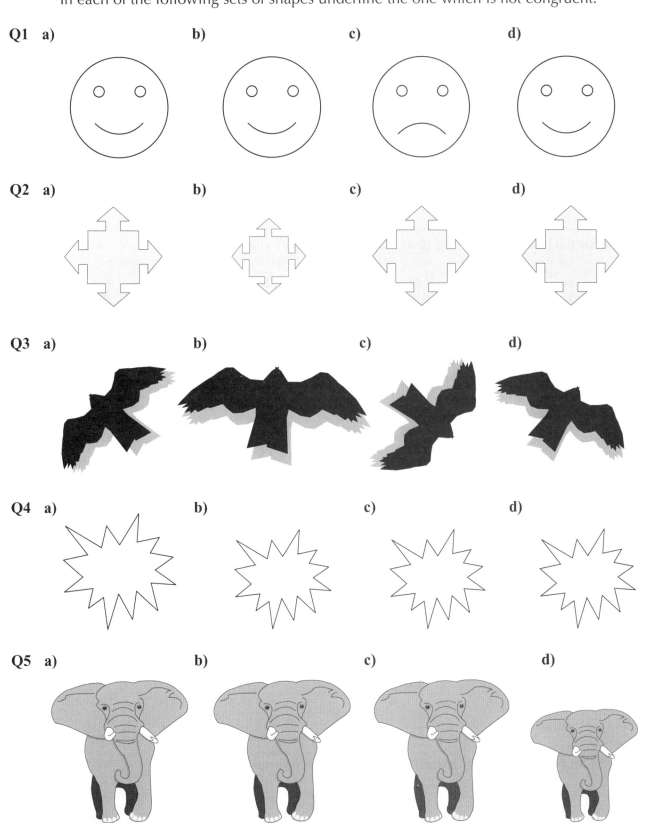

Q1 a) b) c) d)

Q2 a) b) c) d)

Q3 a) b) c) d)

Q4 a) b) c) d)

Q5 a) b) c) d)

81

82

Similarity and Enlargement

Similarity and Scale Factor

Two shapes are <u>similar</u> if they're the <u>same shape</u> but different size. The lengths of the two shapes are related to the scale factor by this very important formula triangle:

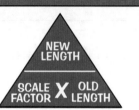

Q1 Two picture frames are shown. One picture is <u>similar</u> to the other. Calculate L cm, the length of the smaller frame.

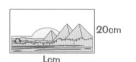

20cm

40 cm

Lcm

50 cm

....

Q2 For each of the following pairs, say with a reason whether the shapes are similar.

i)

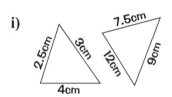

7.5cm

2.5cm 3cm 12cm 9cm

4cm

iii)

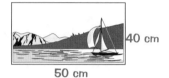

150mm

10mm

15mm 15mm 225mm 225mm

10mm 150mm

....

....

ii)

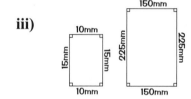

2cm

9cm

78° 48°

48° 78°

5.5cm 3cm

iv)

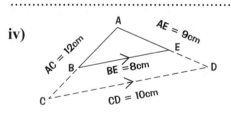

A

AE = 9cm

AC = 12cm E

B BE =8cm D

C CD = 10cm

....

....

Q3 Angle ABC = Angle PQR and Angle BCA = Angle QRP

a) Are the triangles similar? ....

Calculate the following lengths:

b) AB .... **c)** QR ....

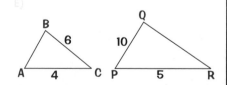

B 6 Q 10

A 4 C P 5 R

Q4 Which of the following must be <u>similar</u> to each other? ....

A Two circles **C** Two rectangles **E** Two equilateral triangles

B Two rhombuses **D** Two squares **F** Two isosceles triangles

SECTION FOUR — ANGLES AND GEOMETRY

Transformations — Enlargements

The scale factor (see previous page) is a fancy way of saying **HOW MUCH BIGGER** the enlargement is than the original. If it's less than 1, it's a reduction. A scale factor of 1/3 means it's reduced to a third of the original size.

Q1   What is the scale factor of each of these enlargements?

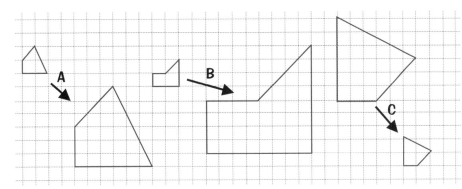

Just pick one of the sides and see how many times longer it is.

A: Scale factor is ....   **B:** Scale factor is ....   **C:** Scale factor is ....

Q2   Enlarge this triangle using scale factor 4 and centre of enlargement C.

Q3 a) Enlarge this shape using scale factor 3 and centre of enlargement E.

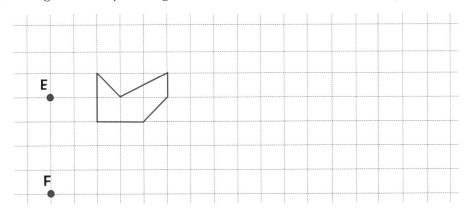

b) Now enlarge the original shape using scale factor 0.5 and centre of enlargement F.

Careful — this is actually a reduction.

Transformations — Enlargements

Q4 The side view of a playground swing is shown in the diagram. Triangle PST is an enlargement of triangle PQR.

a) Write down the distance PT.

....

b) Calculate the distance ST.

....

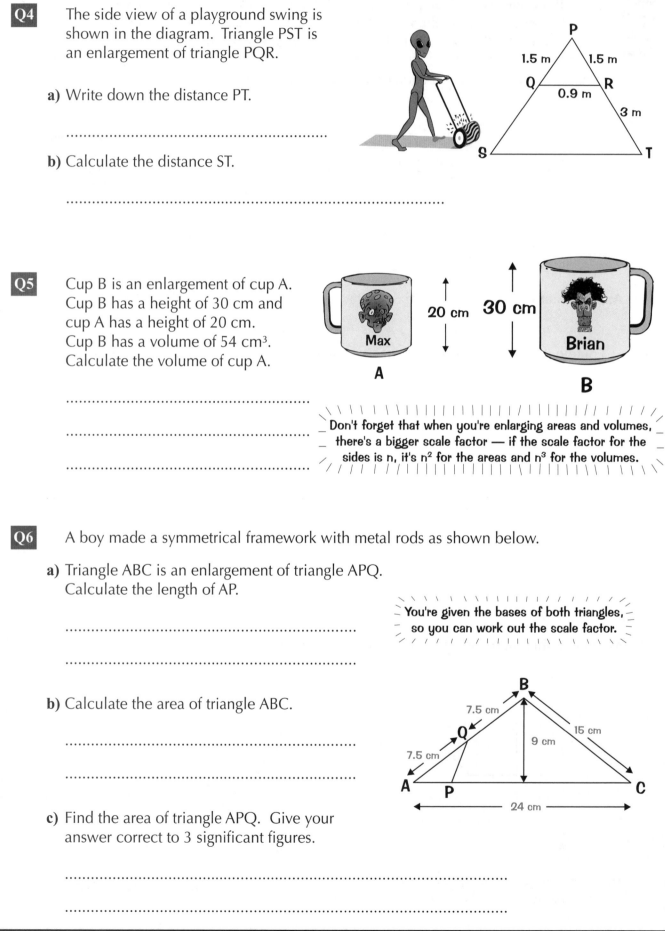

Q5 Cup B is an enlargement of cup A. Cup B has a height of 30 cm and cup A has a height of 20 cm. Cup B has a volume of 54 cm³. Calculate the volume of cup A.

....

....

....

Don't forget that when you're enlarging areas and volumes, there's a bigger scale factor — if the scale factor for the sides is n, it's n² for the areas and n³ for the volumes.

Q6 A boy made a symmetrical framework with metal rods as shown below.

a) Triangle ABC is an enlargement of triangle APQ. Calculate the length of AP.

....

....

You're given the bases of both triangles, so you can work out the scale factor.

b) Calculate the area of triangle ABC.

....

....

c) Find the area of triangle APQ. Give your answer correct to 3 significant figures.

....

....

Transformations — Translation

Translations can be described using <u>vectors</u>.

The vector $\begin{pmatrix} 2 \\ 5 \end{pmatrix}$ means move 2 spaces to the <u>right</u> and 5 spaces <u>up</u>.

The vector $\begin{pmatrix} -3 \\ -4 \end{pmatrix}$ means move 3 spaces to the <u>left</u> and 4 spaces <u>down</u>.

Q1 Translate the shapes A, B and C using these vectors: A $\begin{pmatrix} -4 \\ -3 \end{pmatrix}$ B $\begin{pmatrix} 5 \\ 5 \end{pmatrix}$ C $\begin{pmatrix} 4 \\ -4 \end{pmatrix}$
Label the images A', B' and C'.

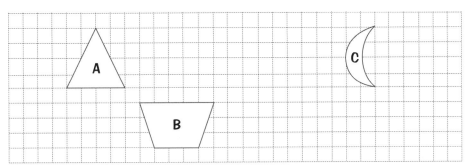

Q2 Translate shape A below using the vectors given in order, drawing the image each time:

P $\begin{pmatrix} 3 \\ 4 \end{pmatrix}$ Q $\begin{pmatrix} 9 \\ 2 \end{pmatrix}$

R $\begin{pmatrix} 3 \\ -4 \end{pmatrix}$ S $\begin{pmatrix} -8 \\ -4 \end{pmatrix}$

Label the images
A', A'' , A''', A''''.

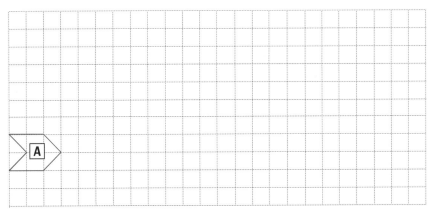

Q3 Write down the <u>translation vectors</u> for the translations shown.

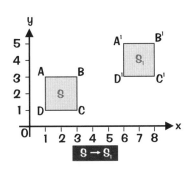

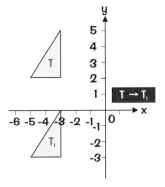

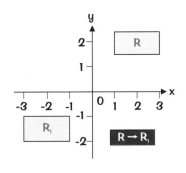

a) ....

b) ....

c) ....

86

Transformations — Reflection

Q1 Reflect each shape in the line x = 4.   **Q2** Reflect the shapes in the line y = x.

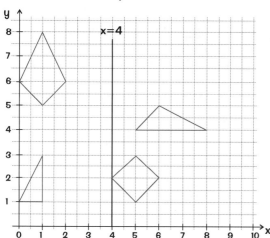

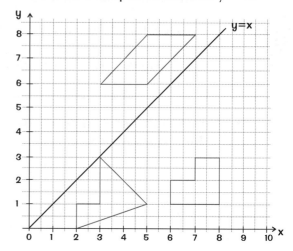

Q3 Reflect ① in the line y = 5, label this ②.

Reflect ② in the line x = 9, label this ③.

Reflect ③ in the line y = x, label this ④.

Reflect ④ in the line x = 4, label this ⑤.

Reflect ⑤ in the line y = x, label this ⑥.

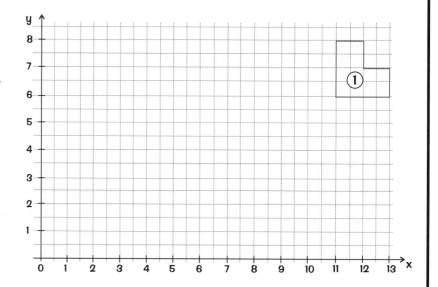

Q4
a) Draw the result of reflecting shape A in the x-axis, label this A′.
b) Draw the result of reflecting shape A′ in the y-axis, label this A″.
c) What single transformation would turn shape A into shape A″?

....

Nothing fancy here, is there? Reflection's just mirror drawing really. And we've all done that before...

SECTION FOUR — ANGLES AND GEOMETRY

Transformations — Rotation

Q1 The centre of rotation for each of these diagrams is **X**. Rotate (turn) each shape as asked then draw the new position of the shape onto each of the diagrams below.

a) 180° (or ½ turn).

b) 270° anticlockwise (or ¾ turn anticlockwise).

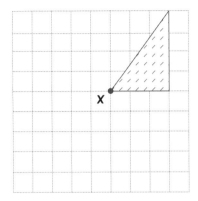

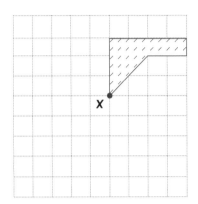

Q2 This is a scalene triangle PQR. The centre of rotation is the origin 0.

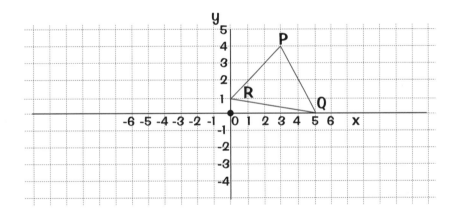

a) Write down the coordinates of...

P .... Q .... R ....

b) Rotate the triangle 90° anticlockwise about the origin 0.
Label the new triangle P′ Q′ R′.

c) Write down the coordinates of ...

P′ .... Q′ .... R′ ....

☞ A ½ *turn clockwise* is the same as a ½ *turn anti-clockwise* — and
a ¼ *turn clockwise* is the same as a ¾ *turn anti-clockwise*. Great fun, innit...

Probability

 When you're asked to find the probability of something, always check that your answer is between 0 and 1. If it's not, you know straight away that you've made a mistake.

Q1   Write down whether these events are impossible, unlikely, even, likely or certain.

   a) You will go shopping on Saturday. ....

   b) You will live to be 300 years old. ....

   c) The next person who comes into the room is female. ....

   d) There will be a moon in the sky tonight. ....

Q2   A bag contains ten balls. Five are red, three are yellow and two are green.
       What is the probability of picking out:

   a) A yellow ball? ....

   b) A red ball? ....

   c) A green ball? ....

   d) A red or a green ball? ....

   e) A blue ball? ....

Q3   Write down the probability of these events happening:

   a) Throwing an odd number with a six-sided dice. ....

   b) Drawing a black card from a pack of playing cards. ....

   c) Drawing a black King from a pack of cards. ....

   d) Throwing a prime number with a six-sided dice. ....

Q4   Mike and Nick play a game of pool. The probability of Nick winning is 7/10.

   a) Put an arrow on the probability line below to show the probability of Nick winning.
       Label this arrow N.

   b) Now put an arrow on the probability line to show the probability of Mike winning the
       game. Label this arrow M.

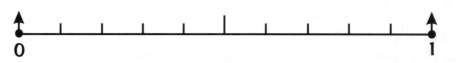

Probability

Q5 The outcome when a coin is tossed is head (H) or tail (T).
Complete this table of outcomes when two coins are tossed together.

a) How many possible outcomes are there? ....

b) What is the probability of getting 2 heads? ....

c) What is the probability of getting a head
followed by a tail? ....

		2ⁿᵈ COIN	
		H	**T**
1ˢᵗ COIN	**H**		
	T		

Q6 Two dice are rolled together. The scores on the dice are added.
Complete the table of possible outcomes below.

How many different combinations are there? ....

	SECOND DICE					
	1	**2**	**3**	**4**	**5**	**6**
1						
2	3					
3						
4						
5			8			
6						

(FIRST DICE)

What is the probability of scoring:

a) 2 ....

b) 6 ....

c) 10 ....

d) More than 9 ....

e) Less than 4 ....

f) An even number ....

g) More than 12 ....

Q7 Two spinners are spun and the scores are multiplied together.

		SPINNER 1	
	2	**3**	**4**
3			
4			
5			

(SPINNER 2)

Fill in this table of possible outcomes.

What is the probability of scoring 12? ....

To win you have to score 15 or more.
What is the probability of winning? ....

In the exam, you might not be asked to put the "possible outcomes" in a table. But it's
a good idea to make your own table anyway — that way you don't miss any out.

Probability

Well, OK, the probability is that you'd rather not be doing these at all...
still — this is the last page, so I'm sure you'll cope for a bit longer.

Q8 One day Sarah did a survey in her class on sock colour. She found out that pupils were wearing white socks, black socks or red socks. Jack said "If I pick someone at random from the class, then the probability that they are wearing red socks is 1/3." Explain why Jack might be wrong.

....

....

Q9 Imagine you have just made a 6-sided spinner in Design and Technology. How could you test whether or not it's a fair spinner?

Remember — if the spinner's fair, the probability of landing on each side is the same.

....

....

....

Q10 a) A biased dice is rolled 40 times. A six came up 14 times. Calculate the relative frequency that a six was rolled.

....

b) The same dice is rolled another 60 times. From this, a six came up 24 times. Calculate the relative frequency that a six was rolled.

....

c) Use the data from a) and b) to make the best estimate you can of the probability of rolling a six with the dice.

....

Q11 "There is a 50% chance that it will rain tomorrow because it will either rain or it won't rain." Is this statement true or false? Explain your answer.

....

....

....

Mode and Median

To find the <u>mode</u>, put the data in order of size first — then it's easier to see which number you've got most of.

Q1 Find the mode for each of these sets of data.

a) 3,   5,   8,   6,   3,   7,   3,   5,   3,   9,

.... Mode is ....

b) 52,   26,   13,   52,   31,   12,   26,   13,   52,   87,   41

.... Mode is ....

Q2 The temperature in °C on 10 Summer days in England was:

25,   18,   23,   19,   23,   24,   23,   18,   20,   19

What was the modal temperature?

.... Modal temperature is .... °C.

Q3 The time it takes thirty pupils in a class to get to school each day in minutes is:

18,   24,   12,   28,   17,   34,   17,   17,   28,   12,   23,   24,   17,   34,   9,
32,   15,   31,   17,   19,   17,   32,   15,   17,   21,   29,   34,   17,   12,   17

What is the modal time?

....

....

Modal time is .... mins.

Put the data in order of size for <u>median</u> questions too — it's much easier to find the middle value.

Q4 Find the median for these sets of data.

a) 3,   6,   7,   12,   2,   5,   4,   2,   9

.... Median is ....

b) 14,   5,   21,   7,   19,   3,   12,   2,   5

.... Median is ....

Q5 These are the heights of fifteen 16 year olds.

162 cm   156 cm   174 cm   148 cm   152 cm   139 cm   167 cm   134 cm
157 cm   163 cm   149 cm   134 cm   158 cm   172 cm   146 cm

What is the median height? Write your answer in the shaded box.

														Median

Mean and Range

Yikes — MEAN questions... well, they're not as bad as everyone makes out.
Remember to include zeros in your calculations — they still count.

Q1 Find the mean of each of the sets of data below. If necessary, round your answers to 1 decimal place:

a) 13, 15, 11, 12, 16, 13, 11, 9 = ...

Remember the formula for mean — total of the items ÷ number of items.

b) 16, 13, 2, 15, 0, 9 = ...

c) 80, 70, 80, 50, 60, 70, 90, 60, 50, 70, 70 = ...

Q2 Find, without a calculator, the mean for each of these sets of data:

a) 5, 3, 7, 3, 2 = ...

b) 7, 3, 9, 5, 3, 5, 4, 6, 2, 6 = ...

Q3 a) Stephen scored a mean mark of 64 in four Maths tests. What was his total mark for all four tests?

....

b) When he did the next test, his mean mark went up to 66.
What mark did he get in the fifth test?

....

Q4 The number of goals scored by a hockey team over a period of 10 games is listed below.

0, 3, 2, 4, 1, 2, 3, 4, 1, 0.

What is the range of the number of goals scored? ....

Q5 Sarah and her friends were measured and their heights were found to be:

1.52 m, 1.61 m, 1.49 m, 1.55 m, 1.39 m, 1.56 m.

What is the range of the heights? ....

Q6 Here are the times 6 people took to do a Maths test:

1 hour 10 mins, 2 hours 10 mins, 1 hour 35 mins,
1 hours 55 min, 1 hour 18 mins, 2 hours 15 mins.

What is the range of these times? ....

Averages

 Geesh — as if it's not enough to make you work out all these boring averages, they want you to write stuff about them as well. Oh well, here goes nothing.

Q1 These are the mathematics marks for John and Mark.

John	65	83	58	79	75
Mark	72	70	81	67	70

Calculate the mean and range for each pupil. Who do you think is the better maths student? Why?

....

....

Q2 Jane has a Saturday job. She earns £3.70 an hour. She thinks that most of her friends earn more. Here is a list of how much an hour her friends are paid.

Lisa £3.60   Scott £4.50   Kate £4.25   Kylie £3.40
Helen £4.01   Kirsty £4.25   Ben £4.25   Ruksana £3.90

Work out the mean, median and mode for her friends' pay.

....

....

Jane's employer offers her a rise to £4.02 because she claims that this is the average hourly rate. Which average has her employer used?

....

Which average should Jane use to try to negotiate a higher pay rise?

....

Q3 The number of absences for 20 pupils during the spring term were:

0 0 0 0 0 0 1 1 1 2 3 4 4 4 7 9 10 10 19 22

Work out the mean, median and modal number of absences.

....

....

If you were a local newspaper reporter wishing to show that the local school has a very poor attendance record, which average would you use and why?

....

If you were the headteacher writing a report for the parents of new pupils, which average would you use and why?

....

Averages

Q4   On a large box of matches it says "Average contents 240 matches".
I counted the number of matches in ten boxes. These are the results:

241   244   236   240   239   242   237   239   239   236

Is the label on the box correct? Use the mean, median and mode for the numbers of
matches to explain your answer.

....

....

Q5   The shoe sizes in a class of girls are:

3   3   4   4   5   5   5   5   6   6   6   7   8

Calculate the mean, median and mode for the shoe sizes.

....

....

If you were a shoe shop manager, which average would be most useful to you, and why?

....

Q6   A house-building company needs a bricklayer.
This advert appears in the local newspaper.
The company employs the following people:

Position	Wage
Director	£700
Foreman	£360
Plasterer	£300
Bricklayer	£250
Bricklayer	£250

Bricklayer wanted
Average wage
over £350 p.w.

What is the median wage?

....

What is the mean wage?   ....

Which gives the best idea
of the average wage?   ....

Is the advert fair? Explain your answer.

Write a fairer advert
in the space above.

....

....

Tally / Frequency Tables

Q1 At the British Motor Show 60 people were asked what type of car they preferred.
Jeremy wrote down their replies using a simple letter code.

Saloon - S   Hatchback - H   4x4 - F   MPV - M   Roadster - R

Here is the full list of replies.

H	S	R	S	S	R	M	F	S	S	R	R
M	H	S	H	R	H	M	S	F	S	M	S
R	R	H	H	H	S	M	S	S	R	H	H
H	H	R	R	S	S	M	M	R	H	M	H
H	S	R	F	F	R	F	S	M	S	H	F

Fill in the tally table and add up the frequency in
each row. Draw the frequency graph of the results.

> **A frequency graph** just means a bar chart.

TYPE OF CAR	TALLY	FREQUENCY
Saloon		
Hatchback		
4 × 4		
MPV		
Roadster		

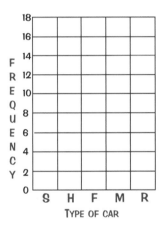

Q2 Last season Newcaster City played 32 matches.
The number of goals they scored in each match were recorded as shown.

2	4	3	5		1	0	0	1
1	0	3	2		1	1	1	0
4	2	1	2		1	3	2	0
0	2	3	1		1	1	0	4

Complete the tally chart and draw the frequency polygon of the goals.

GOALS	TALLY	FREQUENCY
0		
1		
2		
3		
4		
5		

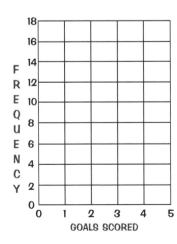

> **A frequency polygon** is
> where you plot points for
> the frequencies and join
> them up with straight lines.

Tally / Frequency Tables

Q3   Here is a list of marks which 32 pupils gained in a History test:

65	78	49	72	38	59	63	44
55	50	60	73	66	54	42	72
33	52	45	63	65	51	70	68
84	61	42	58	54	64	75	63

Complete the tally table making sure you put each mark in the correct group.
Then fill in the frequency column.

MARKS	TALLY	FREQUENCY
31-40		
41-50		
51-60		
61-70		
71-80		
81-90		
	TOTAL	

Q4   The frequency table below shows the number of hours spent Christmas shopping by 100 people surveyed in a town centre.

Number of Hours	0	1	2	3	4	5	6	7	8
Frequency	1	9	10	10	11	27	9	15	8
Hours × Frequency									

a) What is the modal number of hours spent Christmas shopping? ....

b) Fill in the third row of the table.

c) What is the total amount of time spent Christmas shopping by all the people surveyed?

....

d) What is the mean amount of time spent Christmas shopping by a person?

....

Grouped Frequency Tables

As a rule these are trickier than standard frequency tables — you'll certainly have to tread carefully here. Have a good look at the box below and make sure you remember it.

Mean and Mid-Interval Values

1) The <u>MID-INTERVAL VALUES</u> are just what they sound like — the middle of the group.
2) Using the Frequencies and Mid-Interval Values you can estimate the <u>MEAN</u>.

$$\text{Estimated Mean} = \frac{\text{Overall Total (Frequency} \times \text{Mid-interval value)}}{\text{Frequency total}}$$

Shoe Size	1 - 2	3 - 4	5 - 6	7 - 8	Totals
Frequency	15	10	3	1	29
Mid-Interval Value	1.5	3.5	5.5	7.5	—
Frequency x Mid-Interval Value	22.5	35	16.5	7.5	81.5

So the estimated mean value is 81.5 ÷ 29 = 2.81

Q1 In a survey of test results in a French class at Blugdon High, these grades were achieved by the 23 pupils:

(grade) score	(E) 31-40	(D) 41-50	(C) 51-60	(B) 61-70
frequency	4	7	8	4

a) Write down the mid-interval values for each of the groups.

....

b) Calculate an estimate for the mean value.

....

....

Q2 This table shows the number of bowlers, out of a total of 80, who took the wickets in cricket matches over the course of a season.

No. of Wickets	1 - 10	11 - 20	21 - 30	31 - 40	41 - 50	51 - 60	61 - 70	71 - 80	81 - 90	91 - 100
No. of Bowlers	2	3	5	7	19	16	14	10	3	1

a) Write down the modal class. ....

b) Which class contains the median number of wickets?

....

Grouped Frequency Tables

Q3 This table shows times for each team of swimmers, the Dolphins and the Sharks.

Dolphins			Sharks		
Time interval (seconds)	Frequency	Mid-interval value	Time interval (seconds)	Frequency	Mid-interval value
$14 \leq t < 20$	3	17	$14 \leq t < 20$	6	17
$20 \leq t < 26$	7	23	$20 \leq t < 26$	15	23
$26 \leq t < 32$	15		$26 \leq t < 32$	33	
$32 \leq t < 38$	32		$32 \leq t < 38$	59	
$38 \leq t < 44$	45		$38 \leq t < 44$	20	
$44 \leq t < 50$	30		$44 \leq t < 50$	8	
$50 \leq t < 56$	5		$50 \leq t < 56$	2	

a) Complete the table, writing in all mid-interval values.

b) Use the mid-interval technique to estimate the mean time for each team.

....

....

Q4 The lengths of 25 snakes are measured to the nearest cm, and then grouped in a frequency table.

Length	151 - 155	156 - 160	161 -165	166 - 170	171 - 175	Total
frequency	4	8	7	5	1	25

Which of the following sentences may be true and which have to be false?

a) The median length is 161 cm. ....

b) The range is 20 cm. ....

c) The modal class has 7 snakes.

....

d) The median length is 158 cm.

....

> Remember — with grouped data you can't find these values exactly, but you can narrow down the possibilities.

Tables, Charts and Graphs

Q1 Here is a horizontal bar chart showing the favourite colours of a class of pupils.

a) How many like blue best? ....

b) How many more people chose red than yellow? ....

c) How many pupils took part in this survey? ....

d) What fraction of the class prefer green? ....

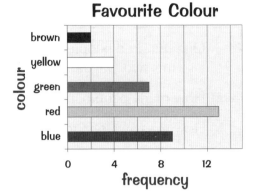

Favourite Colour

Q2 This bar chart shows the marks from a test done by some students:

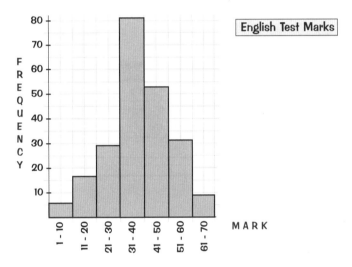

English Test Marks

a) How many students scored 20 marks or less? ....

b) The pass mark for this test was 31. How many students passed the test? ....

c) How many students took the test? ....

Q3 Complete this frequency table, and then draw a bar chart for the results.

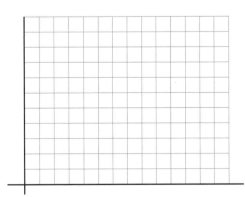

TEST SCORE	TALLY	FREQUENCY
1 - 5	ЖЖ I	6
6 - 10	ЖЖ III	
11 - 15	III	
16 - 20	ЖЖ	
21 - 25	III	

SECTION FIVE — HANDLING DATA

Tables, Charts and Graphs

Make sure you read these questions carefully. You don't want to lose easy marks by looking at the wrong bit of the table or chart.

Q4 One hundred people were asked in a survey what colour eyes they had. Use this two-way table to answer the following questions.

a) How many people in the survey had green eyes? ....

b) How many women took part in the survey? ....

c) How many women had blue eyes? ....

d) How many men had brown eyes? ....

	Green eyes	Blue eyes	Brown eyes	Total
Male	15			48
Female	20		23	
Total		21		100

Q5 This pictogram shows the favourite drinks of a group of pupils.

Favourite Drinks	Number of Pupils
Lemonade	✧ ✧ ✧ ✧ ✧ ✧ ✧ ✧ ✧
Coke	✧ ✧ ✧ ✧ ✧ ✧ ✧ ✧ ✧ ✧ ✧
Tango	✧ ✧ ✧ ✧ ✧ ✧
Orange Squash	✧ ✧ ✧
Milk	✧

✧ Represents 2 pupils.

a) How many pupils were questioned? .... pupils.

b) How many pupils prefer non-fizzy drinks? .... pupils.

c) 18 pupils liked lemonade best. How many more liked coke best? .... pupils.

d) Comment on the popularity of coke compared with milk.

....

Q6 Carol was asked to find out if most people have a calculator in their Maths lessons. She asked the people she liked in her Maths set if they had brought a calculator to school. This table shows their responses:

Yes	No
II	III

From this she claims most people do not have a calculator. Give 3 criticisms of Carol's survey.

....

....

Stem and Leaf Diagrams

Q1 This stem and leaf diagram shows the ages of people in a cinema showing 'The Lord of The Things'.

```
1 | 2 2 4 8 8 9 9
2 | 0 1 1 2 5 6
3 | 0 0 0 5
4 | 2 5 9
5 |
6 | 8
```

Key: 2 | 5 means 25

a) How many people in the cinema were in their twenties? ....

b) Write out the ages of all of the people in the cinema below.

....

Q2 This stem and leaf diagram shows the exam scores of a group of Year 9 pupils.

a) How many pupils got a score between 60 and 70? ....

b) How many scored 80 or more? ....

c) What was the most common test score? ....

d) How many scored less than 50? ....

e) How many pupils took the test? ....

```
3 | 2 3
4 | 6 8 8
5 | 1 2 2 3 6 6 9
6 | 1 5 5 5 8
7 | 2 3 4 5 8
8 | 0 1 1 5
9 | 0 2 3
```

Key: 5 | 2 means 52

Q3 I've been measuring my friends' noses. Here are the lengths in millimetres:

| 12 | 18 | 20 | 11 | 31 |
| 19 | 27 | 34 | 19 | 22 |

Complete the stem and leaf diagram on the right to show the results above.

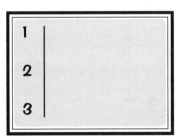

```
1 |
2 |
3 |
```

Key: 2 | 2 means 22

This is nothing new... you've seen it all before. All you do is read off the information from the chart.

Line Graphs

Drawing line graphs is easy — just plot the points,
then join them up with straight lines.

Q1 Billy took his temperature and recorded it on this graph.

What was his temperature at:

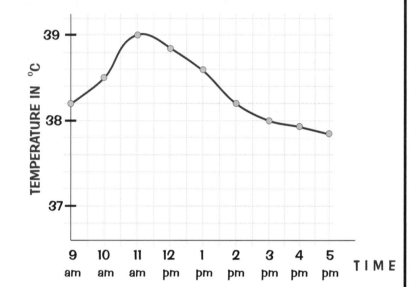

a) 10am? ....

b) 2pm? ....

c) What was his highest
temperature?

....

d) When was this? ....

Q2 A baby was weighed every 5 days. The results are given below. Draw a graph to show how the baby's weight changed.

DAY Nº	0	5	10	15	20	25	30
WEIGHT KG	5.3	5.2	5.9	6.4	6.6	6.7	6.8

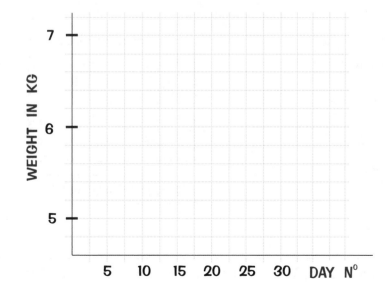

In your own words describe how
the baby's weight changed:

....

....

....

....

Scattergraphs

Q1 These are the shoe sizes and heights for 12 pupils in Year 11.

Shoe size	5	6	4	6	7	7	8	3	5	9	10	10
Height (cm)	155	157	150	159	158	162	162	149	152	165	167	172

On the grid below draw a scattergraph to show this information.

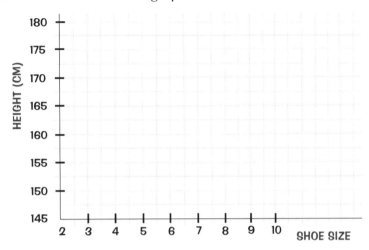

Draw a line of best fit on your scattergraph.

A line of best fit goes through the middle of the points.

What does the scattergraph tell you about the relationship between shoe size and height for these pupils?

....

Q2 The scattergraphs below show the relationship between:

a) The temperature of the day and the amount of ice cream sold.

b) The price of ice cream and the amount sold.

c) The age of customers and the amount of ice cream sold.

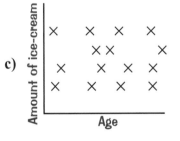

Describe the correlation of each graph and say what each graph tells you.

a)

....

b)

....

c)

....

SECTION FIVE — HANDLING DATA

Scattergraphs

Q3 This scattergraph shows how much time a group of teenagers spend on outdoor activities and playing computer games.

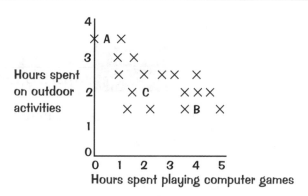

Which of the points A, B or C represent each of these statements?

a)

The rugby practice was a long one so I didn't have much time to play on the computer.

Point ....

b) Point ....

I don't have a computer!

c) Point ....

I went to visit a friend. We played a bit of football then spent most of the evening playing his new computer game.

Q4 Alice wanted to buy a second hand car. She looked in the local paper and wrote down the ages and prices of 15 cars. On the grid below draw a scattergraph for Alice's information.

Age of car (years)	Price (£)
4	4995
2	7995
3	6595
1	7995
5	3495
8	4595
9	1995
1	7695
2	7795
6	3995
5	3995
1	9195
3	5995
4	4195
9	2195

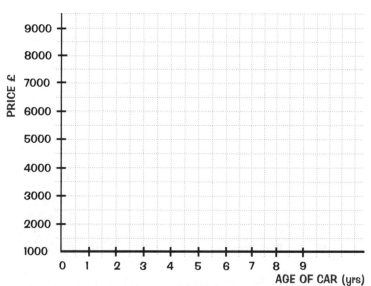

What does the scattergraph tell you about the relationship between the age of a car and its price?

....

The big word you're supposed to use in these questions is **CORRELATION** — and they're very keen on it, so make sure you know what it means.

Pie Charts

Q1 This table shows the daily amount of air time of programme types on TV:

Programme	Hours	Angle
News	5	75
Sport	3	
Music	2	
Current Affairs	3	
Comedy	2	
Other	9	
Total	**24**	

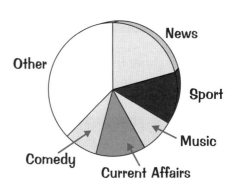

Using an angle measurer, complete the table by finding the size of the angle represented by each type of programme. The first angle is done for you.

Q2 A family spends £540 each week on various items which are listed in the table and shown as sectors on the pie chart. Using an angle measurer, find the angle of each sector and enter it in the table

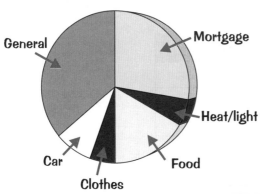

Item	£	Angle
Mortgage	150	
Heat/light	30	
Food	90	
Clothes	30	
Car	45	
General	195	

Pie Charts

Q3 In a University department there are 180 students from different countries.

Country	UK	Malaysia	Spain	Others
Number of students	90	35	10	45

To show this on a pie chart you have to work out the angle of each sector.
Complete the table showing your working. The UK is done for you.

COUNTRY	WORKING	ANGLE in degrees
UK	90 ÷ 180 × 360 =	180°
MALAYSIA		
SPAIN		
OTHERS		

Now complete the pie chart using an angle measurer. The UK sector is done for you.

Q4 Pupils at a school were asked about their activities at weekends. The results are shown in the table. Complete the table and then draw the pie chart using an angle measurer.

ACTIVITY	HOURS	WORKING	ANGLE
Homework	6	6 ÷ 48 × 360 =	45
Sport	2		
TV	10		
Computer games	2		
Sleeping	18		
Listening to music	2		
Paid work	8		
Total	48		

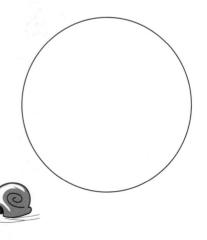

The full circle (that's all 360° of it) represents the total of everything —
so you shouldn't find any gaps in it, basically.

Coordinates

Q1 On the grid plot the following points. Label the points A,B...
Join the points with straight lines as you plot them.

A(0,8) B(4,6) C(4.5,6.5) D(5,6) E(9,8) F(8,5.5) G(5,5) H(8,4) I(7.5,2) J(6,2) K(5,4)
L(4.5,3.5) M(4,4) N(3,2) O(1.5,2) P(1,4) Q(4,5) R(1,5.5) S(0,8).

You should see the outline of an insect. What is it? ....

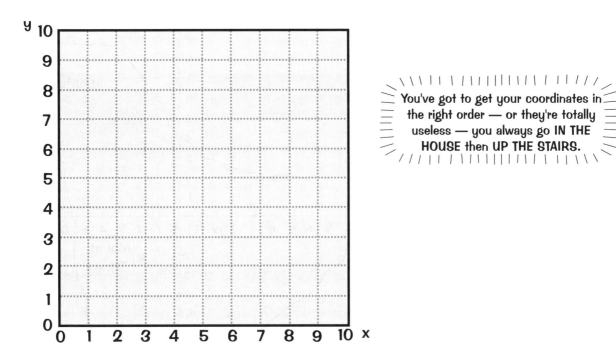

You've got to get your coordinates in the right order — or they're totally useless — you always go IN THE HOUSE then UP THE STAIRS.

Q2 Write down the letter which is by each of the following points.
The sentence it spells is the answer to question one.

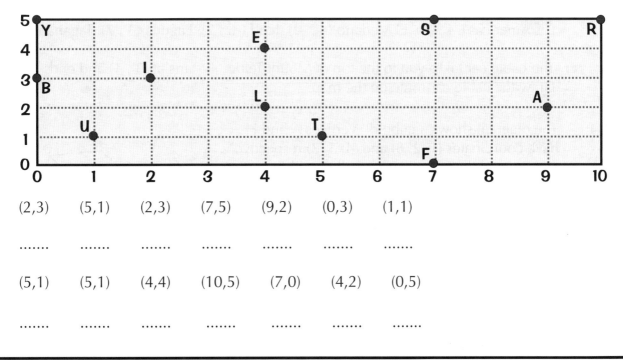

(2,3)   (5,1)   (2,3)   (7,5)   (9,2)   (0,3)   (1,1)

....

(5,1)   (5,1)   (4,4)   (10,5)   (7,0)   (4,2)   (0,5)

....

Coordinates

Q3 The map shows the island of Tenerife where the sun never stops shining...

a) Use the map to write down the coordinates of the following:

Airport (.... , ...)

Mount Teide (.... , ...)

Santa Cruz (.... , ...)

Puerto Colon (.... , ...)

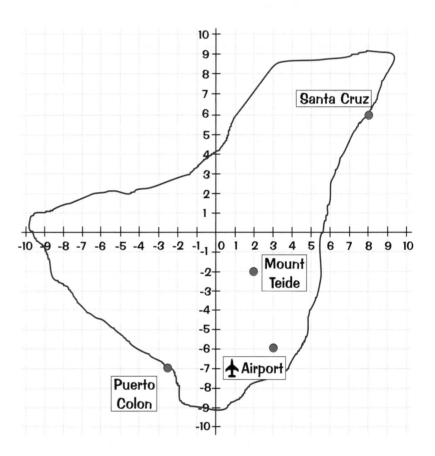

b) Use the coordinates given to mark the following holiday destinations on the map.

Las Americas (-4 , -6), El Medano (4 , -4), Icod (-6 , 2), Laguna (3 , 7), Taganana (9 , 9)

c) The cable car takes you to the top of Mount Teide. It starts at (3 , 1) and ends at (2 , -2). Draw the cable car route on the map.

Q4 The diagram shows a cuboid. Vertices A and H have coordinates (1, 2, 8) and (4, 5, 3) respectively. Write down the coordinates of all the other vertices.

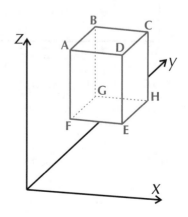

B (.... , ... , ...)

C (.... , ... , ...)

D (.... , ... , ...)

E (.... , ... , ...)

F (.... , ... , ...)

G (.... , ... , ...)

Midpoints of Line Segments

Q1 Find the midpoint of the line segments AB, where A and B have coordinates:

a) A(2,3)   B(4,5)   ....

d) A(3,15)   B(13,3)   ....

b) A(1,8)   B(9,2)   ....

e) A(6,6)   B(0,0)   ....

c) A(0,11)   B(12,11)   ....

f) A(15,9)   B(3,3)   ....

Your answers should be coordinates too.

ahh... nice'n'easy...

Q2 Find the midpoints of each of these line segments:

a) Line segment PQ, where P has coordinates (1,5) and Q has coordinates (5,6).   ....

b) Line segment AB, where A has coordinates (3,3) and B has coordinates (4,0).   ....

c) Line segment RS, where R has coordinates (4,5) and S has coordinates (0,0).   ....

d) Line segment PQ, where P has coordinates (1,3) and Q has coordinates (3,1).   ....

e) Line segment GH, where G has coordinates (0,0) and H has coordinates (–6,–7).   ....

Q3 Find the midpoint of each of the line segments on this graph.

AB: ....

CD: ....

EF: ....

GH: ....

JK: ....

LM: ....

Straight Line Graphs You Should Know

Keep learning these straight lines till they start coming out of your ears — you've got to know about the vertical/horizontal lines and the sloping ones through the origin.

Q1 On the diagram opposite:

a) Label the x axis.
b) Label the y axis.
c) Draw the line x = 3.
d) Draw the line y = 2.

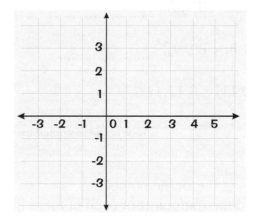

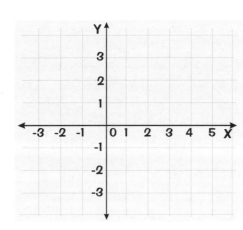

Q2 On the diagram:

a) Label the line x = 0.
b) Label the line y = 0.
c) Draw and label the line y = x.
d) Draw and label the line y = -x.
e) Draw the line x = -3.
f) Draw the line y = -2.

Q3 Which letters represent the following lines:

a) x = y?
b) x = 5?
c) y = -x?
d) x = 0?
e) y = -7?

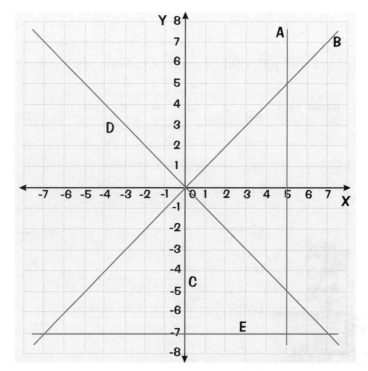

Plotting Straight Line Graphs

The <u>very first thing</u> you've got to do is work out a <u>table of values</u>.

Example: Draw the graph of y = 3x − 1 for values of x
between 0 and 4.

1) First complete a <u>table of values</u>:

x	0	1	2	3	4
y	-1	2	5	8	11

⟸ decided by the question

⟸ worked out using y = 3x - 1

2) Draw the axes.
3) Plot the points.
4) Draw a straight line through the points.

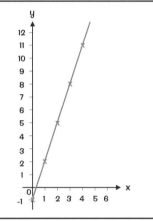

Q1 On the grid shown,
draw axes with x from 0 to 8
and y from 0 to 14.

Q2 a) Complete the table of values,
for y = x + 2.

x	0	1	2	3	4	5	6
y	2			5			

b) Use your <u>table of values</u> to draw the
graph of y = x + 2 on the grid opposite.

Q3 a) Complete the table below,
for y = 2x + 1

x	0	1	2	3	4	5	6
y	1				9		

b) Use your <u>table of values</u> to draw the
graph y = 2x + 1 on the grid opposite.

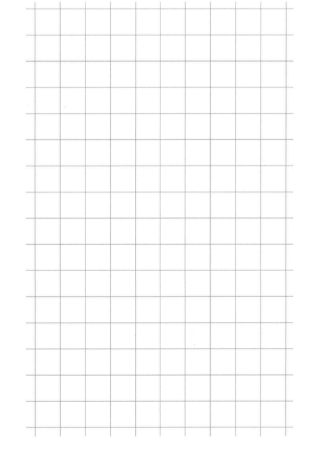

Q4 a) Fill in the table for y = 8 − x,
using values of x from 0 to 6.

x							
y							

b) Draw the graph of y = 8 − x.

Gradients of Lines

The gradient of a line is just a measure of the slope.
The box below tells you everything you need to know about it...

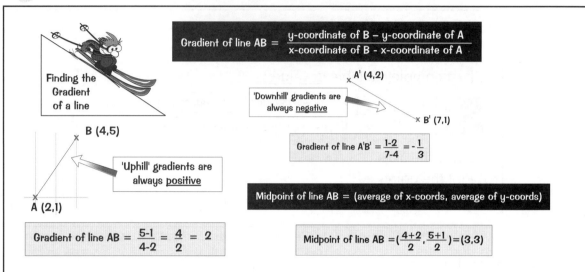

Q1 Draw axes with x from -9 to 9 and y from -12 to 12. On this set of axes join each pair of points and work out the gradient and the midpoint of the line.

A is (1, 1), B is (2, 4)

gradient of AB = ...

midpoint of AB = ...

C is (5, 5), D is (7, 0)

gradient of CD = ...

midpoint of CD = ...

E is (-7, 7), F is (-2, 10)

gradient of EF = ...

midpoint of EF = ...

G is (-6, 2), H is (-3,-4)

gradient of GH = ...

midpoint of GH = ...

I is (-8,-9), J is (-3,-6)

gradient of IJ = ...   midpoint of IJ = ...

Straight Line Graphs: $y = mx + c$

The equations of most straight line graphs can be written in the form:

$$y = mx + c$$

The number multiplying the x term tells you the **gradient** of the graph

The number by itself tells you where the graph crosses the y axis. This is the **y-intercept**

Q1 The following are equations of linear graphs. <u>Without plotting</u> the graphs, state the <u>gradient</u> of each graph and the <u>y-intercept</u>.

a) $y = 4x + 2$ ....

b) $y = 5x - 1$ ....

c) $y = 6x$ ....

d) $y = 5 + 2x$ ....

e) $y = 12 - 3x$ ....

f) $y = x$ ....

g) $y = 3 - x$ ....

h) $y + 2x = 10$ ....

i) $2y = x + 4$ ....

j) $y + 5 = 4x$ ....

Q2 Find the values for m and c if the linear graph $y = mx + c$ has a gradient of 3 and passes through (0, 8).

....

Q3 Find the values for m and c if the linear graph $y = mx + c$ has a gradient of 1 and passes through (2, 0).

....

Finding the Equation of a Straight Line

Now you know how to find the gradient, you can go
a couple of steps further and find the equation of a line.

STEP 1: Work out the gradient of the line, call this 'm'.

STEP 2: Find where the graph crosses the y-axis, call this 'c',

STEP 3: Put your values into the formula $y = mx + c$ — and that's it!

Q1 For each of these lines, find the gradient, m, and the y-intercept, c.
Hence write down the <u>equation</u> of the line.

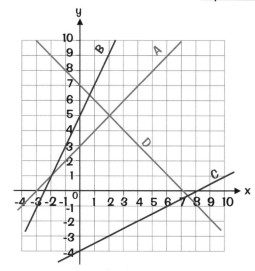

<u>Line A:</u>

m = ..., c = ...

equation is ....

<u>Line B:</u>

m = ..., c = ...

equation is ....

<u>Line C:</u>

m = ..., c = ...

equation is ....

<u>Line D:</u>

m = ..., c = ...

equation is ....

Q2 On the axes shown, draw the <u>straight line</u>
which passes through A(1, 2) and B(5, 4).
Find its gradient (m), y-intercept (c) and
use this to write down its equation.

c = ..., m = ...

equation is ....

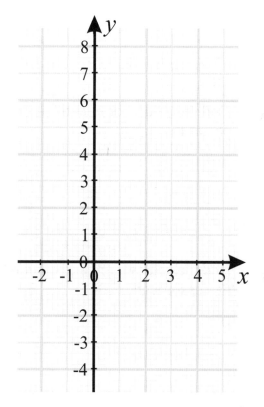

Q3 On the same axes, draw the line passing
through points P (-2,-4) and Q (4, 8).
Find its gradient (m), y-intercept (c) and
use this to write down its equation.

c = ..., m = ...

equation is ....

Quadratic Graphs

Quadratic Graphs

If an expression has an x^2 term in it, it's quadratic. The graphs you get from quadratic expressions are always curves with a certain shape...

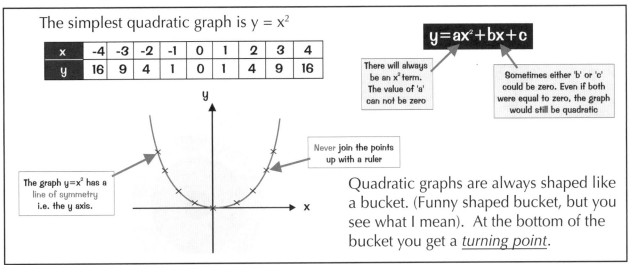

The simplest quadratic graph is $y = x^2$

x	-4	-3	-2	-1	0	1	2	3	4
y	16	9	4	1	0	1	4	9	16

$$y=ax^2+bx+c$$

There will always be an x^2 term. The value of 'a' can not be zero

Sometimes either 'b' or 'c' could be zero. Even if both were equal to zero, the graph would still be quadratic

Never join the points up with a ruler

The graph $y=x^2$ has a line of symmetry i.e. the y axis.

Quadratic graphs are always shaped like a bucket. (Funny shaped bucket, but you see what I mean). At the bottom of the bucket you get a *turning point*.

You'll need some graph paper for the questions on this page.

Q1 Complete this <u>table of values</u> for the quadratic graph $y = 2x^2$.

a) On your graph paper, draw axes with x from -4 to 4 and y from 0 to 32.

b) Plot these 9 points and join them with a <u>smooth curve</u>.

x	-4	-3	-2	-1	0	1	2	3	4
$y=2x^2$	32	18					8		

Remember to square first then x 2

Q2 Complete this table of values for the graph $y = x^2 + x$.

x	-4	-3	-2	-1	0	1	2	3	4
x^2	16	9					4		
$y=x^2+x$	12					2			

By putting more steps in your table of values, the arithmetic is easier

a) Draw axes with x from -4 to 4 and y from 0 to 20.

b) Plot the points and join them with a smooth curve.

c) Draw the <u>line of symmetry</u> for the quadratic graph $y = x^2 + x$, and label it.

d) Use your graph to find the two solutions of the equation $x^2 + x = 0$.

x = ... or ....

Just find the x-values where the graph crosses the x-axis (i.e. where y = 0).

SECTION SIX — GRAPHS

Quadratic Graphs

Q3 **a)** Complete this table of values for the graph $y = x^2 - 4x + 1$.

b) Plot the graph $y = x^2 - 4x + 1$, using axes with x from -2 to 5 and y from -3 to 13.

x	-2	-1	0	1	2	3	4
x^2	4	1				9	
-4x	8					-12	
1	1	1				1	
$y=x^2-4x+1$	13	6				-2	

c) Draw and label the <u>line of symmetry</u>.

d) Use your graph to find approximate solutions of the equation $x^2 - 4x + 1 = 0$.

x = ... or ....

If the x^2 term has a <u>minus</u> sign in front of it, the bucket will be turned <u>upside down</u>.

Q4 **a)** Complete this table of values for the graph $y = 3 - x^2$.

b) Draw the graph $y = 3 - x^2$ for x from -4 to 4.

x	-4	-3	-2	-1	0	1	2	3	4
3	3	3	3	3	3	3	3	3	3
$-x^2$	-16						-4		
$y=3-x^2$	-13						-1		

c) Use your graph to find approximate solutions of the equation $3 - x^2 = 0$.

x = ... or ....

Q5 **a)** Draw the graph $y = -x^2 + x + 4$ for values of x from -3 to 4.
b) Use your graph to find approximate solutions to the equation $-x^2 + x + 4 = 0$

x = ... or ....

If any points look a bit strange, check you've got them right in the <u>table of values</u>. I know it's boring doing it all again, but it shouldn't be too hard if you've put all the steps in. And it'll mean you <u>don't get it wrong</u>. Which is always nice.

Simultaneous Equations with Graphs

The solution of two simultaneous equations is simply the X and Y values where their graphs cross

1) Simultaneous equations can be plotted as two <u>straight-line graphs</u> on the <u>same axes</u>.

2) The point where the lines cross will have <u>coordinates</u> equal to the <u>values of x and y</u> which satisfy both equations.

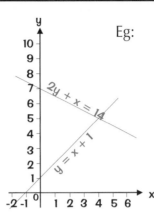

Eg: Solve:
$y = x + 1$
$2y + x = 14$

The two lines <u>intersect</u> where <u>x = 4</u> and <u>y = 5</u>, so this is the solution.

Q1 Solve these simultaneous equations by looking at the graphs.
Then check your answers by substituting the values back into the equations.

a) $y + 2x = 9$ Solution:
$3y = x + 6$
x = ..., y = ...

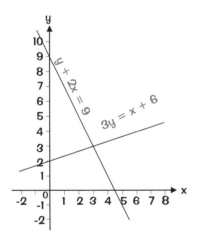

c) $y = x + 6$ Solution:
$3y + x = 18$
x = ..., y = ...

b) $y = 2x + 14$ Solution:
$2y = 8 - x$
x = ..., y = ...

d) $y + x = 1$ Solution:
$3y = x + 11$
x = ..., y = ...

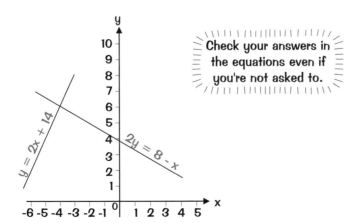

Check your answers in the equations even if you're not asked to.

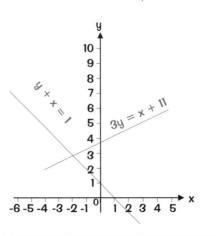

Simultaneous Equations with Graphs

This is a nice easy way of solving simultaneous equations. All you have to be able to do is draw two straight line graphs and read off a value where they cross each other. That means you've got to be up to speed with your straight line graphs, though...

For each pair of simultaneous equations below:

a) draw and label a pair of axes with x from –3 to 7, and y from –6 to 6
b) complete the two tables of values
c) plot two straight-line graphs onto your axes, remembering to label each graph
d) use your graphs to find the value of x and y
e) check your answers by substituting them into both of the equations.

Q2
y = x + 2
y = 3x − 2

	x	−2	0	4
y = x+2		0	2	

	x	0	1	2
y = 3x−2		−2		

x = ...

y = ...

Q3
y = 2x − 2
2y = x + 8

	x			
y = 2x-2				

	x			
y = ½x+4				

x = ...

y = ...

Interpreting Graphs

Q1 Using the <u>conversion graph</u> convert the following to km, rounding your answers to the <u>nearest km</u>:

a) 5 miles ....

c) 11 miles ....

b) 20 miles ....

d) 23 miles ....

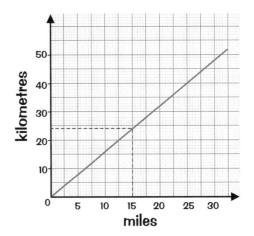

Q2 Change the following to <u>miles</u>, rounding your answers to the nearest mile:

a) 10 km ....

c) 27 km ....

b) 20 km ....

d) 35 km. ....

Q3 Match the following graphs with the statements below:

a) The cost of hiring a plumber <u>per hour</u> including a <u>fixed call-out fee</u>. ....

b) <u>Exchange rate</u> between Euros and American Dollars ....

c) <u>Speed against time</u> for a car travelling at constant speed. ....

d) The <u>area of a circle</u> as the radius increases. ....

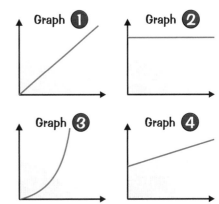

Q4 Water is poured into each of these containers at a <u>constant rate</u>.

Match the containers to the graphs showing the <u>depth</u> of water (d) against <u>time</u> (t) taken to fill the container.

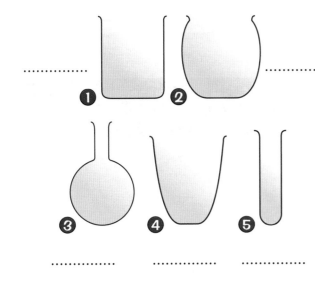

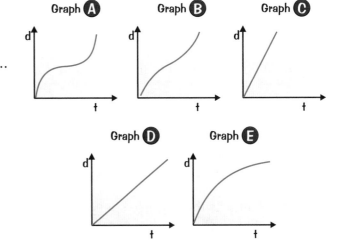

Travel Graphs

Q1 The graph shows Nicola's car journey from her house to Alan's house, picking up Robbie on the way.

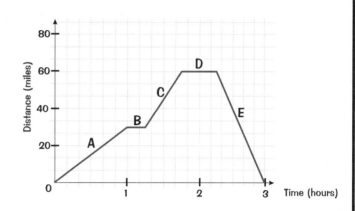

a) If Nicola started her trip at 10.00 am at what time did she return home? ....

b) How far is Robbie's house from Nicola's? ....

c) How long did they stop at Alan's for? ....

d) During which section was the speed greatest? ....

e) How long did the return journey take? ....

f) What was the speed of the car during section E? ....

> You can work out where the houses are by looking for the flat parts of the graph — the bits where Nicola stops. There are two flat parts here — one for Robbie's house and one for Alan's.

Q2 The travel graph shows the journey of a boy going on a run.

a) Between what times was the boy running the <u>fastest</u>?

....

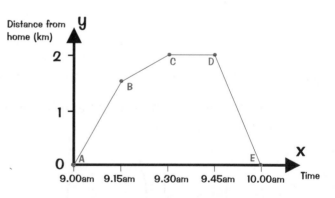

b) Calculate his <u>fastest speed</u> in km/hr.

....

c) For how long was the boy <u>resting</u>?

....

d) What happened to the boy's speed at <u>B</u>?

....

e) How <u>far</u> did the boy run?

....

f) What was the <u>average speed</u> for his entire run?

....

Negative Numbers

Q1 Write these numbers in the correct position on the number line below:

a) −4   3   2   −3   −5   1

0

b) Which temperature is lower (colder), 8 °C or −4 °C ? ....

c) Which temperature is 1° warmer than −24 °C ? ....

Put the correct symbol, < or >, between the following pairs of numbers:

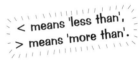

< means 'less than'.
> means 'more than'.

d) 4   −8

e) −6   −2

f) −8   −7

g) −3   −6

h) −1   1

i) −3.6 −3.7

j) Rearrange the following numbers in order of size, largest first:

−2   2   0.5   −1.5   −8   ....

k) If the temperature is 6 °C but it then gets colder and falls by 11 °C, what is the new temperature?

....

l) One day in winter the temperature at 0600 was −9 °C. By midday, it had risen to −1 °C.
By how many degrees did the temperature rise?

....

Negative Numbers

When you've got really big numbers, drawing a number line will still help. But just mark off the tens (or even just the hundreds) — you'll be there all day otherwise.

Answer these questions <u>without</u> using your calculator.

Q2 Work out:

a) 2 – 7 = ...

b) 4 – 18 = ...

c) 1 – 20 = ...

d) 12 – 14 = ...

e) 72 – 77 = ...

f) 3 – 100 = ...

Q3 Work out:

a) -6 + 1 = ...

b) -10 + 2 = ...

c) -8 + 8 = ...

d) -70 + 3 = ...

e) -100 + 13 = ...

f) -1000 + 1 = ...

Q4 Work out:

a) -2 + 5 = ...

b) -6 + 10 = ...

c) -2 + 50 = ...

d) -12 + 100 = ...

e) -47 + 56 = ...

f) -49 + 98 = ...

Q5 Work out:

a) -3 – 2 = ...

b) -3 – 6 = ...

c) -13 – 3 = ...

d) -50 – 4 = ...

e) -2 – 19 = ...

f) -7 – 96 = ...

Standard Index Form

Writing very big (or very small) numbers gets a bit messy with all those zeros. That's if you don't use this standard index form. But, of course, the main reason for knowing about standard form is...you guessed it — it's in the Exam.

Any numbers written in Standard Index Form always look like:

This number must be between 1 and 10 but never equal to 10 → **a x 10ⁿ** ← This number is equal to the number of places the decimal point moves. n is +ve for larger numbers n is -ve for small numbers

eg.
$$5800000000000000000 = 5.8 \times 10^{17}$$
$$43000000000000000000 = 4.3 \times 10^{19}$$
$$0.0000000000000017 = 1.7 \times 10^{-15}$$
$$0.00000000000000008 = 8 \times 10^{-17}$$

Q1 Complete the two tables below.

Number	Standard form
4500000000	
19300000000000	
	8.2×10^{12}
82000000	
	6.34×10^{8}
	4.02×10^{6}
423400000000	
	8.431×10^{7}
	1.03×10^{5}
4700	

Number	Standard form
0.000000006	
0.00000000072	
	8.5×10^{-6}
0.000000143	
	7.12×10^{-5}
	3.68×10^{-10}
	4.003×10^{-8}
0.0000009321	
	5.2×10^{-3}
	9.999×10^{-7}
0.00000000802	
	2.3104×10^{-6}
0.000001	

Q2 Find the value of the following, giving your answers in standard form.

a) $46 \times 4.2 \times 5000 =$ ....

b) $20 \times 40 \times 50 \times 8.2 =$ ....

c) $0.2 \times 0.3 \times 0.5 \times 0.1 =$ ....

d) $5000 \div 0.02 =$ ....

e) $62000 \div 0.31 =$ ....

f) $40000000 \div 1000 =$ ....

Standard Index Form

Q3 Rewrite the following, either in standard form or by changing standard form to normal numbers.

a) Mercury is 694000000 km from the Sun.

....

b) The Sahara desert covers 8600000 km^2.

....

c) The Earth is approximately 4.5×10^9 years old.

....

d) The average depth of the Atlantic is 3.7×10^3 metres.

....

e) The charge on an electron is 1.6×10^{-19} Coulombs.

....

f) A Uranium nucleus can release 3.20×10^{-11} Joules of energy.

....

g) In Chemistry, Avogadro's constant is 6.033×10^{23}.

....

h) The length of the Earth's equator is 40076 km.

....

i) The population of the USA is approximately 249231000 people.

....

j) From Washington to Tokyo is 6763 miles.

....

k) A tonne of coal can produce 2.8×10^{10} Joules of energy.

....

l) The radius of the nucleus of an atom is 0.0000000000003 cm.

....

You've got to remember the formula a × 10^n. To find n, count the number of spaces the decimal point moves. If the number you're converting is large, n is positive. If it's small, n is negative. And don't forget, a has to be between 1 and 10. Easy as cake...

Standard Index Form

This stuff gets a lot easier if you know how to handle your calculator — read and learn.

Standard Index Form with a Calculator

Use the **EXP** button (or **EE** button) to enter numbers in standard index form.

Eg $1.7 \times 10^9 + 2.6 \times 10^{10}$ **1** **.** **7** **EXP** **9** **+** **2** **.** **6** **EXP** **10** **=**

The answer is **2.77**^{10} which is read as 2.77×10^{10}

Q4 What is <u>7 million</u> in standard index form?

Q5 Which is <u>greater</u>, 4.62×10^{12} or 1.04×10^{13}, and by how much?
....

Q6 Which is <u>smaller</u> 3.2×10^{-8} or 1.3×10^{-9} and by how much?
....

Q7 The following numbers are <u>not</u> written in standard index form.
Rewrite them correctly using standard index form.

  a) 42×10^6 ....   **d)** 11.2×10^{-5} ....

  b) 38×10^{-5} ....   **e)** 843×10^3 ....

  c) 10×10^6 ....   **f)** 42.32×10^{-4} ....

Q8 One atomic mass unit is equivalent to 1.661×10^{-27} kg. What are
<u>two</u> atomic mass units equivalent to (in standard index form)?
....

Q9 The radius of the Earth is 6.38×10^3 km. What is the radius of
the Earth measured in <u>cm</u>? Leave your answer in standard form.
....

Q10 The length of a light year, the distance light can travel in one year, is 9.461×10^{15} m.
Write <u>in standard form</u> the distance that light can travel in:

  a) 2 years ....   **b)** 6 months ....

Q11 If $x = 4 \times 10^5$ and $y = 6 \times 10^4$ work out the value (in standard index form) of

  a) xy ....   **b)** 4x ....   **c)** 3y ....

Don't forget — when you're using a calculator, you've got to write the
answer as **3.46 $\times$ 10^{27}**, <u>not</u> as **3.46^{27}**. If you do it the wrong way,
it means something <u>completely</u> different.

Powers

Q1 Complete the following:

a) $2^4 = 2 \times 2 \times 2 \times 2 =$ ....

b) $10^3 = 10 \times 10 \times 10 =$ ....

c) $3^5 = 3 \times$ .... $=$ ....

d) $4^6 = 4 \times$ .... $=$ ....

e) $1^9 = 1 \times$ .... $=$ ....

f) $5^6 = 5 \times$ .... $=$ ....

Q2 Simplify the following:

a) $2 \times 2 \times 2 \times 2 \times 2 \times 2 \times 2 \times 2 =$ ....

b) $12 \times 12 \times 12 \times 12 \times 12 =$ ....

c) $m \times m \times m =$ ....

d) $y \times y \times y \times y =$ ....

Q3 Use your <u>calculator</u> to find the exact value of

a) 4^3 ....   **b)** 10^4 ....   **c)** 12^5 ....   **d)** 13^3 ....

Q4 Complete the following (the first one has been done for you):

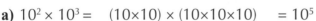

a) $10^2 \times 10^3 =$ $(10 \times 10) \times (10 \times 10 \times 10)$ $= 10^5$

b) $10^3 \times 10^4 =$ .... $=$

c) $10^4 \times 10^2 =$ .... $=$

d) What is the <u>quick method</u> for writing down the final result in **b)** and **c)**?

....

Q5 Complete the following (the first one has been done for you):

a) $2^4 \div 2^2 = \dfrac{(2 \times 2 \times 2 \times 2)}{(2 \times 2)} = 2^2$

c) $4^5 \div 4^3 = \dfrac{(4 \times 4 \times 4 \times 4 \times 4)}{\text{....................}} =$ ....

b) $2^5 \div 2^2 = \dfrac{(2 \times 2 \times 2 \times 2 \times 2)}{(2 \times 2)} =$ ....

d) $8^5 \div 8^2 = \dfrac{\text{....................}}{\text{....................}} =$ ....

e) What is the quick method for writing down the final result in **b)**, **c)** and **d)**?

....

You can always write out all the 10s or whatever if you get stuck.

Q6 Write the following as a <u>single term</u>:

a) $10^6 \div 10^4 =$ ....

b) $(8^2 \times 8^5) \div 8^3 =$ ....

c) $6^{10} \div (6^2 \times 6^3) =$ ....

d) $x^2 \times x^3 =$ ....

e) $a^5 \times a^4 =$ ....

f) $p^4 \times p^5 \times p^6 =$ ....

Powers are just a way of writing numbers in shorthand — they come in especially handy with big numbers. Imagine writing out 2^{138} — $2 \times 2 \times... \times 2 \times... \times 2 \times$ yawn $\times$ zzz...

Square and Cube Roots

Square root just means "WHAT NUMBER TIMES ITSELF (i.e. 2×2) GIVES..."
The square roots of 64 are 8 and –8 because 8×8=64 and -8×-8=64.

Cube root means "WHAT NUMBER TIMES ITSELF TWICE (i.e. 2×2×2) GIVES ..."
The cube root of 27 is 3 because 3×3×3=27.

Square roots always have a + and – answer, cube roots only have 1 answer.

Tip

Q1 Use the $\sqrt{}$ button on your calculator to find the following <u>positive</u> square roots to the nearest whole number.

a) $\sqrt{60}$ = ...

b) $\sqrt{19}$ = ...

c) $\sqrt{34}$ = ...

d) $\sqrt{200}$ = ...

e) $\sqrt{520}$ = ...

f) $\sqrt{75}$ = ...

g) $\sqrt{750}$ = ...

h) $\sqrt{0.9}$ = ...

i) $\sqrt{170}$ = ...

j) $\sqrt{7220}$ = ...

k) $\sqrt{1000050}$ = ...

l) $\sqrt{27}$ = ...

Q2 Without using a calculator, write down both answers to each of the following:

a) $\sqrt{4}$ = ...

b) $\sqrt{16}$ = ...

c) $\sqrt{9}$ = ...

d) $\sqrt{49}$ = ...

e) $\sqrt{25}$ = ...

f) $\sqrt{100}$ = ...

g) $\sqrt{144}$ = ...

h) $\sqrt{64}$ = ...

i) $\sqrt{81}$ = ...

Q3 Use your calculator to find the following:

a) $\sqrt[3]{4096}$ = ...

b) $\sqrt[3]{1728}$ = ...

c) $\sqrt[3]{1331}$ = ...

d) $\sqrt[3]{1000000}$ = ...

e) $\sqrt[3]{1}$ = ...

f) $\sqrt[3]{0.125}$ = ...

Q4 Without using a calculator, find the value of the following:

a) $\sqrt[3]{64}$ = ...

b) $\sqrt[3]{512}$ = ...

c) $\sqrt[3]{125}$ = ...

d) $\sqrt[3]{1000}$ = ...

e) $\sqrt[3]{216}$ = ...

f) $\sqrt[3]{8000}$ = ...

Q5 A square rug has an area of 400 m². What is the length of an edge?

....

Q6 A solid cube puzzle has a volume of 343 cm³. Find the length of one of its edges.

....

Number Patterns and Sequences

Q1   Draw the next two pictures in each pattern.
How many match sticks are used in each picture?

a)

....

b)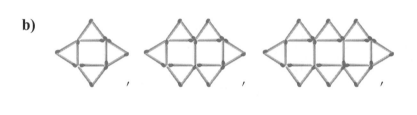

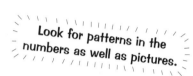

Look for patterns in the numbers as well as pictures.

....

,

....

c)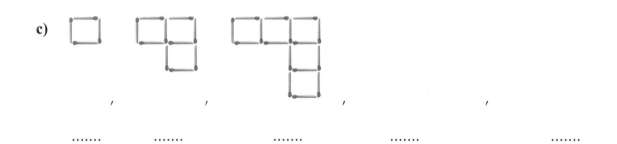

,   ,   ,   ,

....

Q2   Look for the pattern and then fill in the next three lines. Some of the answers are too big to fit on a calculator display so you must spot the pattern.

a)   7 × 6   = 42

67 × 66   = 4422

667 × 666   = 444222

6667 × 6666   = ...

66667 × 66666   = ...

666667 × 666666 = ...

b)   1 × 81 = 81

21 × 81 = 1701

321 × 81 = 26001

4321 × 81 = 350001

54321 × 81 = ...

654321 × 81 = ...

7654321 × 81 = ...

Number Patterns and Sequences

Q3 In each of the questions below, write down the next three numbers in the sequence and write the rule that you used.

Once you've worked out the next numbers, go back and write down exactly what you did — that will be the rule you're after.

a) 1, 3, 5, 7, ... , ... , ... Rule ....

b) 2, 4, 8, 16, ... , ... , ... Rule ....

c) 3, 30, 300, 3000, ... , ... , ... Rule ....

d) 3, 7, 11, 15, ... , ... , ... Rule ....

e) 19, 14, 9, 4, –1, ... , ... , ... Rule ....

Q4 The letter n describes the position of a term in the sequence. For example, if $n = 1$, that's the 1st term…if $n = 10$ that's the 10th term and so on.
In the following, use the rule given to generate (or make) the first 5 terms.

a) $3n + 1$ so if $n = 1$ the 1st term is $\underline{(3 \times 1) + 1} = \underline{4}$

   $n = 2$ the 2nd term is .... = ...

   $n = 3$ .... = ...

   $n = 4$ .... = ...

   $n = 5$ .... = ...

b) $5n - 2$, when $n = 1, 2, 3, 4$ and 5
   produces the sequence .... , ... , ... , ... , ...

c) n^2, when $n = 1, 2, 3, 4$, and 5
   produces the sequence .... , ... , ... , ... , ...

d) $n^2 - 3$, when $n = 1, 2, 3, 4$, and 5
   produces the sequence .... , ... , ... , ... , ...

Q5 Write down an expression for the nth term of the following sequences:

a) 2, 4, 6, 8, …
   ....

   Remember the formula —
   $dn + (a - d)$.

b) 1, 3, 5, 7, …
   ....

c) 5, 10, 15, 20, …
   ....

d) 5, 8, 11, 14, …
   ....

Formulas from Words

It's no big mystery — algebra is just like normal sums, but with the odd letter or two stuck in for good measure.

Q1   Write the algebraic expression for these:

a) Three more than x ....

b) Seven less than y ....

c) Four multiplied by x ....

d) y multiplied by y ....

e) Ten divided by b ....

f) A number add five ....

Q2   Steven is 16 years old. How old will he be in:

a) 5 years? ....

b) 10 years? ....

c) x years? ....

Q3   Tickets for a football match cost £25 each. What is the cost for:

a) 2 tickets? ....

b) 6 tickets? ....

c) y tickets? ....

CGP Wanderers Football Club
Vs United Rovers FC

Comfy Seat
East stand lower bit
Row 20
Seat 104

£25.00

Q4   There are n books in a pile. Write an expression for the number of books in a pile that has:

a) 3 more books ....

b) 4 fewer books ....

c) Twice as many books ....

Q5 **a)** I have 6 CDs and I buy 5 more. How many CDs have I now? ....

b) I have 6 CDs and I buy *w* more. How many CDs have I now? ....

c) I have x CDs and I buy *w* more. How many CDs have I now? ....

Q6 **a)** This square has sides of length 3 cm.

What is its perimeter? ....

What is its area? ....

3 cm

3 cm

b) This square has sides of length d cm.

What is its perimeter? ....

What is its area? ....

d cm

d cm

Rearranging Formulas

Rearranging is getting the letter you want out of the
formula and making it the subject.

Example:- Rearrange the formula $p = 3q + r$ to make q the subject.

$p = 3q + r$

$p - r = 3q$ — Subtract r from each side

$\dfrac{p - r}{3} = q$ — Divide by 3

$q = \dfrac{p - r}{3}$ — Rewrite starting with new subject

Remember
The same method applies
to rearranging formulas
as solving equations

Q1 Rearrange the following formulas to make the <u>letter in brackets</u> the new subject:

a) $y = x + 4$ (x)

d) $a = 7b + 10$ (b)

g) $y = 3x + \frac{1}{2}$ (x)

b) $y = 2x + 3$ (x)

e) $w = 14 + 2z$ (z)

h) $y = 3 - x$ (x)

c) $y = 4x - 5$ (x)

f) $s = 4t - 3$ (t)

i) $y = 5(x + 2)$ (x)

Q2 Rearrange the following, to make the <u>letter in brackets</u> the subject of the formulas:

a) $y = \dfrac{x}{10}$ (x)

e) $f = \dfrac{3g}{8}$ (g)

b) $s = \dfrac{t}{14}$ (t)

f) $y = \dfrac{x}{5} + 1$ (x)

c) $a = \dfrac{2b}{3}$ (b)

g) $y = \dfrac{x}{2} - 3$ (x)

d) $d = \dfrac{3e}{4}$ (e)

h) $a = \dfrac{b}{3} - 5$ (b)

Q3 A car sales person is paid £w for working m months
and selling c cars, where $w = 500m + 50c$.
a) Rearrange the formula to make <u>c the subject</u>.
b) Find the number of cars the sales person sells
in 11 months if he earns £12,100 during that time.

Q4 The rectangle has length l cm and width w cm. Its perimeter is p cm.

a) Write down a <u>formula</u>
with p as the subject.
b) Rearrange this to make l the subject.
c) Find the length of a rectangle of
width 7.5 cm and perimeter 44 cm.

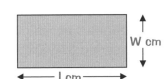

SECTION SEVEN — ALGEBRA

132

Substituting Values into Formulas

BODMAS — this funny little word helps you remember in which order to work formulas out. The example below shows you how to use it. Oh and by the way "Other" might not seem important, but it means things like powers and square roots, etc — so it is.

Example: if $z = \frac{x}{10} + (y-3)^2$, find the value of z when x = 40 and y = 13.

1) Write down the formula with the numbers stuck in, $z = \frac{40}{10} + (13-3)^2$

2) <u>B</u>rackets first: $z = \frac{40}{10} + (10)^2$

3) <u>O</u>ther next, so square: $z = \frac{40}{10} + 100$

4) <u>D</u>ivision before <u>A</u>ddition: $z = 4 + 100$

$\underline{z = 104}$

Q1 If x = 3 and y = 6 find the value of the following expressions.

a) x + 2y .... **c)** 4(x + y) .... **e)** $2x^2$ ....

b) 2x ÷ y .... **d)** $(y - x)^2$ .... **f)** $2y^2$ ....

Q2 If V = lwh, find V when, **a)** l = 7, w = 5, h = 2 ....

b) l = 12, w = 8, h = 5. ....

Q3 Using the formula $z = (x - 10)^2$, find the value of z when,

a) x = 20 .... **b)** x = 15 .... **c)** x = -1 ....

Q4 If V = u + at, find the <u>value of V</u> when u = 8, a = 9.8 and t = 2. ....

Q5 The cost, C pence, of hiring a taxi depends on the number, n, of miles you travel in it, where C = 100 + 25n. Find C when

a) n = 2 .... **b)** n = 10 .... **c)** n = 15 ....

Q6 The cost of framing a picture, C pence, depends on the <u>dimensions of the picture</u>. If C = 10L + 5W, where L is the length in cm and W is the width in cm, then find the cost of framing:

a) a picture of length 40 cm and width 24 cm ....

b) a square picture of sides 30 cm. ....

Q7 The time taken to cook a chicken is given as 20 minutes per lb plus 20 minutes extra. Find the time needed to cook a chicken weighing:

a) 4 lb ....

b) 7.5 lb ....

You need to write your own formula for this one.

SECTION SEVEN — ALGEBRA

Algebra — Collecting Terms and Expanding

Algebra can be pretty scary at first. But don't panic — the secret is just to practise lots and lots of questions. Eventually you'll be able to do it without thinking, just like riding a bike. But a lot more fun, obviously...

Simplifying means collecting like terms together:	_Expanding_ means removing brackets:
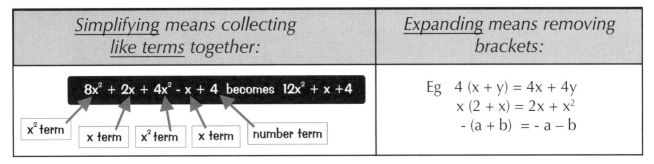	Eg $4(x + y) = 4x + 4y$ $x(2 + x) = 2x + x^2$ $-(a + b) = -a - b$

Q1 By collecting like terms, simplify the following. The first one is done for you.

a) $6x + 3x - 5 = 9x - 5$

b) $2x + 3x - 5x =$ ....

c) $9f + 16f + 15 - 30 =$ ....

d) $14x + 12x - 1 + 2x =$ ....

e) $3x + 4y + 12x - 5y =$ ....

f) $11a + 6b + 24a + 18b =$ ....

g) $9f + 16g - 15f - 30g =$ ....

h) $14a + 12a^2 - 3 + 2a =$ ....

Q2 Simplify the following. The first one is done for you.

a) $3x^2 + 5x - 2 + x^2 - 3x = 4x^2 + 2x - 2$

b) $5x^2 + 3 + 3x - 4 =$ ....

c) $13 + 2x^2 - 4x + x^2 + 5 =$ ....

d) $7y - 4 + 6y^2 + 2y - 1 =$ ....

e) $2a + 4a^2 - 6a - 3a^2 + 4 =$ ....

f) $15 - 3x - 2x^2 - 8 - 2x - x^2 =$ ....

g) $x^2 + 2x + x^2 + 3x + x^2 + 4x =$ ....

h) $2y^2 + 10y - 7 + 3y^2 - 12y + 1 =$ ....

Q3 Expand the brackets and then simplify if possible. The first one is done for you.

> Careful with the minus signs — they multiply both terms in the bracket.

a) $2(x + y) = 2x + 2y$

b) $4(x - 3) =$ ....

c) $8(x^2 + 2) =$ ....

d) $-2(x + 5) =$ ....

e) $-(y - 2) =$ ....

f) $x(y + 2) =$ ....

g) $x(x + y + z) =$ ....

h) $8(a + b) + 2(a + 2b) =$ ....

Algebra — Expanding Double Brackets

It's best to stick to this method — otherwise you're bound to miss one of the terms.

To multiply out double brackets use <u>FOIL</u>:	
<u>F</u>irst — Multiply the first terms in each bracket <u>O</u>utside — Multiply the outside terms <u>I</u>nside — Multiply the inside terms <u>L</u>ast — Multiply the last terms	Eg $(x + 2)(3x - 4)$ $= (x \times 3x) + (x \times -4) + (2 \times 3x) + (2 \times -4)$ $= 3x^2 - 4x + 6x - 8$ $= 3x^2 + 2x - 8$

Q1 For each of the large rectangles below,
write down the <u>area</u> of the four smaller rectangles.

a)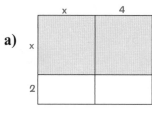

b)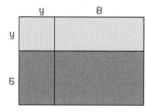

c)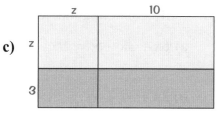

.... ' .... ' .... ' ....

.... ' .... ' .... ' ....

Q2 Multiply out the brackets and simplify your answers where possible:

a) $(x + 4)(x + 2)$

....

b) $(y + 8)(y + 5)$

....

c) $(z + 10)(z + 3)$

....

(Use your answers to **Q1** to help you check you've multiplied out the brackets correctly.)

Q3 Expand the brackets and simplify:

a) $(x + 1)(x + 2) =$ **d)** $(x + 5)(x - 1) =$

b) $(x + 3)(x + 2) =$ **e)** $(2x + 2)(x - 3) =$

c) $(x + 4)(x + 5) =$ **f)** $(x - 3)(3x + 1) =$

Algebra — Expanding Double Brackets

Q4 For each large rectangle write down the area of the four <u>small</u> rectangles, and hence find an <u>expression</u> for the area of the <u>large</u> rectangle.

a)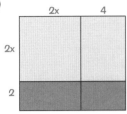

....
....
....
....

b)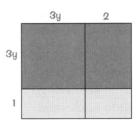

....
....
....
....

c)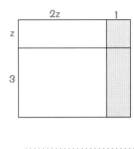

....
....
....
....

Q5 By expanding the brackets, simplify the following:

a) $(2x + 1)(2x + 2)$ ....

b) $(2x + 3)(x + 1)$ ....

c) $(3x + 2)(3x + 4)$ ....

d) $(3x + 1)(x + 2)$ ....

e) $(2x - 1)(2x - 2)$ ....

f) $(2x - 3)(2x - 2)$ ....

g) $(3x - 1)(3x - 1)$ ....

h) $(4x - 2)(4x - 3)$ ....

i) $(2 + 2x)(2x - 1)$ ....

j) $(3 + 2x)(x - 2)$ ....

Algebra — Taking out Common Factors

$$7x^2 + 21xy = 7x(x + 3y)$$

| largest number that will go into 7 and 21 | highest power of x, that will go into each term | y is not in every term so it is not a common factor, and goes inside the brackets |

Q1 Factorise the expressions below. Each has <u>4</u> as a common factor.

a) $4x + 8$ = ...

c) $4 - 16x$ = ...

b) $12 - 8x$ = ...

d) $4x^2 + 64$ = ...

Q2 Factorise the expressions below. Each has <u>7</u> as a common factor.

a) $21 - 7x$ = ...

c) $14 + 21x$ = ...

b) $28x + 7$ = ...

d) $35x^2 - 14$ = ...

Q3 Factorise the expressions below. Each has <u>x</u> as a common factor.

a) $2x + x^2$ = ...

c) $x - 16x^2$ = ...

b) $2x - x^2$ = ...

d) $4x^2 - 3x$ = ...

Q4 Factorise the expressions below. Each has <u>2x</u> as a common factor.

a) $2x + 4x^2$ = ...

c) $2x - 16x^2$ = ...

b) $2x - 8x^3$ = ...

d) $4xy - 6x^2$ = ...

Q5 Factorise the expressions below by taking out any <u>common factors</u>.

a) $2x + 4$ = ...

f) $30 + 10x$ = ...

b) $3x + 12$ = ...

g) $9x^2 + 3x$ = ...

c) $24 + 12x$ = ...

h) $5x^2 + 10x$ = ...

d) $16x + 4y$ = ...

i) $7x^2 + 21x$ = ...

e) $3x + 15$ = ...

j) $3y + xy^2$ = ...

First look for any numbers the terms have in common, then look for the letters.

Solving Equations

You've got to get the letter on its own (x = ...).
You can add, divide... well, anything really — but you gotta
do it to both sides or it'll all go horribly wrong.

Q1 Solve these equations:

a) a + 6 = 20

b) b + 12 = 30

c) 48 + c = 77

....

....

....

d) 397 + d = 842

e) e + 9.8 = 14.1

f) 3 + f = 7

....

....

....

Q2 Solve these equations:

a) g – 7 = 4

b) h – 14 = 11

c) i – 38 = 46

....

....

....

d) j – 647 = 353

e) k – 6.4 = 2.9

f) l – 7 = -4

....

....

....

Q3 Solve these equations:

a) 4m = 28

b) 7n = 84

c) 15p = 645

....

....

....

d) 279q = 1395

e) 6.4r = 9.6

f) -5s = 35

....

....

....

Q4 Solve these equations:

a) $\dfrac{t}{3} = 5$

b) u ÷ 6 = 9

c) $\dfrac{v}{11} = 8$

....

....

....

d) $\dfrac{w}{197} = 7$

e) x ÷ 1.8 = 7.2

f) $\dfrac{y}{-3} = 7$

....

....

....

Solving Equations

These are just like the last page... only there's an extra step.
It's a good idea to get rid of any fractions before you do anything else.

Q5   Solve these equations:

a) $3x + 2 = 14$

                  ....

b) $5x - 4 = 31$

                  ....

c) $8 + 6x = 50$

                  ....

d) $20 - 3x = -61$

                  ....

Q6   Solve these equations:

a) $\frac{x}{3} + 4 = 10$

                  ....

b) $\frac{x}{5} - 9 = 6$

                  ....

c) $4 + \frac{x}{9} = 6$

                  ....

d) $\frac{x}{17} - 11 = 31$

                  ....

> For help with these, look back over <u>expanding brackets</u> and <u>collecting like terms</u>.

Q7   Solve these equations:

a) $3(2x + 1) = 27$

                  ....

b) $2(4x + 1) + x = 56$

                  ....

c) $5x + 3 = 2x + 15$

                  ....

d) $2(x + 7) = 6x - 10$

                  ....

Q8   Solve the following:

a) $3(7 - 2x) = 2(5 - 4x)$

                  ....

b) $4(3x + 2) + 3 = 3(2x - 5) + 2$

                  ....

c) $6(x + 2) + 4(x - 3) = 50$

                  ....

d) $10(x + 3) - 4(x - 2) = 7(x + 5)$

                  ....

Trial and Improvement

Q1 Use the trial and improvement method to solve the equation $x^3 = 50$.
Give your answer to one decimal place. Two trials have been done for you.

Try $x = 3$ $x^3 = 27$ (too small)
Try $x = 4$ $x^4 = 64$ (too big)

....

Q2 Use the trial and improvement method to solve these equations.
Give your answers to one decimal place.

a) $x^2 + x = 80$

....

b) $x^3 - x = 100$

....

Show all the numbers you've tried, not just your final answer...
or you'll be chucking away easy marks.

Inequalities

Yet another one of those bits of Maths that looks worse than it is —
these are just like equations, really, except for the symbols.

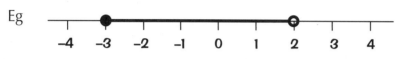

The 4 Inequality Symbols:

> means greater than   < means less than
⩾ means greater than or equal to   ⩽ means less than or equal to

Inequalities can be represented on number lines. You need to know this notation, too:

Eg

$$-4 \quad -3 \quad -2 \quad -1 \quad 0 \quad 1 \quad 2 \quad 3 \quad 4$$

REMEMBER:
● includes the value
○ does not include it

represents the inequality $-3 \leqslant x < 2$

Q1 Write down an inequality for each of the diagrams below.

a)

-1 0 1 2 3 4 5   ....

b)

-2 -1 0 1 2 3 4   ....

c)

8 9 10 11 12 13 14   ....

d)

-4 -3 -2 -1 0 1 2   ....

e)

-7 -6 -5 -4 -3 -2 -1   ....

f)

0 1 2 3 4 5 6   ....

g)

-3 -2 -1 0 1 2 3   ....

h)

-17 -16 -15 -14 -13 -12 -11   ....

i)

20 21 22 23 24 25 26   ....

j)

-2 -1 0 1 2 3 4   ....

k)

-1 0 1 2 3 4 5   ....

l)

-3 -2 -1 0 1 2 3   ....

Q2 Solve the following inequalities:

a) $2x \geqslant 16$ ....

b) $4x > -20$ ....

c) $x + 2 > 5$ ....

d) $x - 3 \leqslant 10$ ....

e) $x + 4 \geqslant 14$ ....

f) $10x > -2$ ....

g) $5 + x \geqslant 12$ ....

h) $x/4 > 10$ ....

i) $x/3 \leqslant 1$ ....

j) $x/2 \leqslant 4$ ....

k) $5x + 4 < 24$ ....

l) $5x + 7 \leqslant 32$ ....

m) $3x + 12 \leqslant 30$ ....

n) $2x - 7 \geqslant 8$ ....

o) $17 + 4x < 33$ ....

Q3 There are <u>1,130</u> pupils in a school and no classes have more
than <u>32</u> pupils. What is the least number of <u>classrooms</u> that
could be used? Show this information as an inequality.

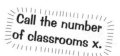
Call the number of classrooms x.

....

MFW42